The Trail Life

How I Loved it, Hated it, and Learned from it

Julie Urbanski

The Trail Life: How I Loved it, Hated it, and Learned from it

ISBN: 1468023128
ISBN-13: 978-1468023121

Self-published by Julie Urbanski
Images, artwork and editing provided by Julie Urbanski
www.urbyville.com

First Edition

DEDICATION

To Urbyville and all of its present and future residents and guests.

CONTENTS

PREFACE

We are ever-changing beings. We change so much that when we look back on our old selves, through pictures or in reading journals of a time forgotten, we almost don't recognize the person we used to be, for better or for worse. Writing this book was an attempt to take a snapshot of who I was and what I was thinking in my late twenties, as a Pacific Crest Trail thru-hiker that had a life-changing experience and was trying to cope with everything that happened not only during the hike, but in the ensuing years of truly digesting the meaning of the hike. I will never be that person ever again. Nor will I think the same as that person, because life demands that we continually change how we think and act, requiring a new skin each and every day.

This book is a reflection of realizations that occurred to me both while I hiked and shortly afterwards while I acclimated myself to the real world of work, bills and responsibilities. It takes aspects from life on the trail, like the simple act of drinking water, and not only portrays that piece of the trail life to the reader, but also applies it to everyday life, making connections that make us more aware of our surroundings, our actions, and our mindsets.

Though many people could benefit from the mental and physical strengthening of a thru-hike, it is simply not feasible for the majority because of the requirements of time, money, and the basic desire to endure such a feat. This book is for such people that may never hike a single mile, who appreciate life-changing experiences because of the revelations they allow for and the connections they make to our daily actions, thoughts and relationships.

The trail life was a raw experience, with life lessons that slapped me in the face and left me crying without so much as an explanation or an apology. It was a life stripped of comforts and technology, but because of the absence of such things, it allowed for incredible clarity in seeing the building blocks of living out a happy, fulfilled life. The upcoming pages reveal such lessons, organized from basic to complex, along with how they appeared throughout the trail and how they are implemented in our daily lives. While these lessons are not unique to the trail, the trail life uniquely portrays the lessons that oftentimes get lost in the shuffle of our daily cobweb of to-do lists and deadlines. They are lessons that are easily understood, yet not always on the front burner of our mind; rather than being taped to the fridge as a daily reminder, they get shoved in the junk drawer, never to surface again.

I was not a hiker before stepping foot on the Pacific Crest Trail, nor do I even consider myself outdoorsy to this day. I partake in adventures such as this because of the gauntlet my mind and body must go through in order to come out a better person on the other end, and though I came away with hundreds of photos as a testament of this journey, they don't tell the whole story. The story of the trail life: how it's lived, why it matters, and what it means for the improvement of me and the lives of those that read about it.

1 YOU DID WHAT?

In the summer of 2007, I set out to walk from Mexico to Canada along the Pacific Crest National Scenic Trail. Over 2,600 miles on one continuous path, in one single trip. Also known as thru-hiking.

Yes, there were signs to follow and no, I did not do it alone. I carried my belongings on my back, slept outside, pooped in the woods, and walked all day for 109 continuous days.

The entire adventure was experienced with my then-boyfriend, Matt. Although it was all my decision to expose myself to such a life for over three months, that decision was not without heavy persuasion from Matt. He convinced me to take that first step on what some call "the long brown ribbon," otherwise known as the Pacific Crest Trail. From here on out, the PCT.

When I first heard about the PCT, I thought Matt was making things up. He prefaced its existence with stories from his experience thru-hiking the Appalachian Trail, the AT. The AT is another long-distance hiking trail that ambles through woods and backcountry, covering over 2100 miles from Georgia to Maine. I soon likened the PCT to the West Coast counterpart to the AT. Before I met him, Matt had successfully thru-hiked the AT in 2000 and had the book of pictures to prove it. Since he was proud of his feat, he never failed to take trips down memory lane with the photos and I perused that photo book at least five times within the first year I knew him. The tangible proof convinced me that such a life existed.

When I finally believed in the PCT's existence and in the validity of Matt's claims that people actually chose to walk it, most often after hiking the AT, I thought to myself, "Good luck barking up that tree, buddy, because there's no way I would ever do something like that."

My history of camping thus far had involved sleepovers in the backyard in my grade school years, and even those ended up inside once we all got scared. Instead of revealing my thoughts to him, I smiled and flipped the next pages of pictures, wondering how long I'd stay with a guy that willingly and excitedly chose a life outside.

That was around the year 2003, when I first met Matt. It had been three years since he had thru-hiked the AT. In trail years, three years is forever between thru-hiking two trails. Most people who enjoy thru-hiking can barely go a season, much less years, without the itch to get back out on the trail. Only the good memories seem to float to the top, even if they cursed every step along the way, no matter how much they told themselves during the hellish walk, "Never again." That phrase somehow becomes, "Maybe it would be different next time if I…" Next thing they know they're at the start of another trail with a heavy pack and weak legs.

Since I had yet to ever complete my first trail, I was of the mindset that I'd never be convinced to even start one. I didn't have the itch to hike like Matt did. The idea of thru-hiking was easily dismissible, even laughable. I was the first to bring it up as a joke. Yet, as our relationship carried on, the more Matt talked about hiking the PCT with that sparkle in his eyes, the more my laugh turned into a nervous grumble. I knew that he actually believed I might say yes one day, and we're not talking about *that* question. Oh no, once Matt had the trail on his mind, nothing else mattered.

One thing that many people do not know about Matt is that he is the master of the slow-drip method of persuasion. He's not an in-your-face kind of salesman. Rather, he's the subtle kind that leads you to believe you came up with the entire idea yourself. All the time that you believe the idea started with you, he is the one that planted the seed and harvested it right under your feet. He accomplishes this through the slow-drip method.

Wholly unbeknown to the poor person being subjected to his persuasion, he drops hints for an adventure such as hiking the PCT. Each drop amounts to the size of a droplet of water, similar to those from a leaky bathroom faucet. The drops are seemingly harmless at first and barely audible when they hit the sink. Yet, those droplets quickly become a big deal when you either can't sleep at night because the sound is invading your sleep, or when you get the water bill and realize that something really should be done about that drip.

Matt's endless hints about hiking the PCT finally got to me in the winter of 2006, when we were living in Annapolis, Maryland. We were deciding what to do with ourselves after his upcoming completion of graduate school in the spring of 2007. Somehow, I don't know how, the PCT made its way into the mix of possibilities. Graduation was in May, obligations were few past that point, and a reserve of money had been saved. Most importantly, we had slowly amassed hiking gear that just happened to be perfect for a long-distance trail.

"Ugh," is what I really thought when I realized his sneaky plan. It was when I had finally received the water bill and realized that I had let enough water drip to amount to a small pond.

Great. Just enough to drown in.

With a great sigh and a rolling of the eyes, I agreed with Matt, who was excited beyond belief, that the PCT was a possibility in the spring of 2007. Phone calls were made to old trail friends from the AT, Ron and Dan, aka Rocketcop and Animal. More hiking gear suddenly showed up in corners of the bedroom. I knew that the term "possibility" sky-rocketed the trail to the top of the list. I also knew the only way I was getting out of the trail was to break up with Matt or break a bone, preferably one I needed to walk. While sitting on my cozy couch in the winter of 2006, wrapped in a fleece blanket and cupping a bowl of ice cream, the idea of hiking a trail sounded much better than ending a relationship just because I didn't want to walk. Being a long-distance runner, I questioned how much harder walking all day could be compared to running a marathon, and I thought that running would at least help my physical and mental ability to hike. I'll break the news early and spoil the surprise: it didn't.

Weeks later, when Rocketcop and Animal joined the PCT-bound group, I knew my fate. I knew there was no turning back, no matter what other options I thought of for the spring of 2007. I knew I would either make it or break up with Matt in trying.

In both preparing for the trail and in actually hiking it, I often wondered, "Who in the world thought of this awful thing?" Ashamed as I am to admit it, I cursed both the creators and the trail's existence during my life on the trail. I had a hard time believing good people in the world created such a thing for the actual enjoyment of others. I honestly thought that most people incarcerated, on drugs, or in some other way delinquent with the law, should hike the trail for their punishment. Even today, after having finished it, I still partially agree with myself. Only after completing the hike was I able to appreciate all the efforts from the past and present trail aficionados that have made such an influential part of my life possible.

The PCT covers a measly three states (how hard can that be?), including California, Oregon and Washington, spanning over 2600 miles. According to the Pacific Crest Trail Association, the trail started out as several disconnected trails, with people first exploring routes for the trail in the 1920s and 1930s. Several men were instrumental in hatching and implementing the idea of a continuous trail from Mexico to Canada. Thank goodness I did not know their names while hiking the trail. I just might have yelled those names out loud during a difficult, rocky ascent in the Sierra Nevada or during one of the many pop-up rain storms deep in the Northern Cascades of Washington. A few expletives may have been involved as well.

Clinton Clarke and Warren Rogers are credited with lobbying hard with the federal government for the trail's existence, and though its completion wasn't seen for years, decades of efforts from other key trail supporters eventually made such a trail possible today.

After years of proposed trails, routes, and maps, the 1968 National Trails Systems Act established the PCT, among other national scenic trails. Still, many years passed before an official route came to be. Lapses of decades were due to disagreements between the government and private land owners regarding the placement of the trail's path. Those disagreements still continue today. The trail was officially dedicated in the summer of 1993. I was only eleven years old then and had no idea how significantly that date would affect my life over a decade later. It is a date that represents the completion of a major part of my life.

And so I have influential men from the course of the trail's history, along with the unseen efforts of so many others both before and after them, to thank for one of my life's greatest experiences. While I may not have thought so while hiking, I learned more about myself and the world than I had ever dared to conceive possible. On the particularly hard days on the trail, usually when I was craving a Sunkist soda or a bag of potato chips, I would think to myself, "Where would I be if this thing were never created?"

I can finally answer with confidence, "Nowhere better."

Anyone can hike the PCT, no matter their age, education, background or circumstances. There was an eleven-year-old and his father hiking the trail the same year as myself, and the pair had already conquered the AT together. To say that I felt like a wimp as I cried myself to sleep some nights is an understatement, as I would remember that there was a mere child out there passing over the same difficult terrain.

A unique feature of long-distance hiking is that hikers get a new name, a trail name. It's like a rebirth when starting a thru-hike. In a life experience that changes a person both inside and out, trail names are aptly fitting. A person goes through so many physical and mental transformations along the trail that he is in a sense a different person from the time his feet greet the trail to the time he again reaches pavement for good. And I'm not talking normal names, like Mike, John, Sarah, or Kim. I'm talking Optimist, Out of Order, No Car, Rocketcop, Prozac and Stopwatch. Interesting names that carry meaning and that elicit pride in that meaning.

People are usually named based on circumstances, personality traits, or just dumb luck. Matt and Dan became Optimist and Animal on the AT because they each wore a t-shirt that read "Optimist" for Matt, and "Animal" for Dan. Though their names weren't creative beyond their choice of clothing, they were certainly fitting. Matt, here on out known as Optimist, kept that name through the years and no doubt used it again on the PCT. I never found out most people's real names on the trail. It would have been strange to call them anything other than their trail name. To this day, Rocketcop is Rocketcop. I cringe when I say his real name, Ron, because it just sounds wrong. Features like trail names make the trail life all the more unique and enticing to those who join such a niche group of people.

None of this answers how a thru-hike is actually carried out once the first step is taken. In case there is any confusion, a thru-hike is when a long-distance trail is completed in one fell swoop, from point A to point B. A hiker can go as fast or as slow as he wants, can walk as many miles as he wants each day, and has few restrictions as to what he needs to do each day. The to-do list is short and the time spent crossing off the items is up to the hiker to decide. Walking, a hiker's biggest to-do item, is also the most time consuming, so the range of time required to do so varies greatly from hiker to hiker.

To an outsider, it is a dream of a life. Responsibilities are merely to oneself, the only schedules or deadlines are self-imposed, and never once does the alarm clock wake a hiker to the morning commute to the office. There's hardly even an awareness of which day is which, whether it's a weekday or the weekend. To a hiker, they are all the same. It is a wonderful life until the walking starts and doesn't end until Canada. Despite the simplicity of the action, walking is by no means an easy task. A lot of people quit walking well before the border.

Success rates for completing a thru-hike are low for many reasons. The Pacific Crest Trail Association indicates that the percentage of people who tend to complete the PCT thru-hike is around sixty percent, with about three hundred people starting the trail each year. With what I now know about the hike, even that percentage sounds too high. Thru-hiking is extremely hard, both physically and mentally, and a lot of people just can't handle the challenges posed by long-distance backpacking. I found that out on the first day when all I wanted to do was quit and resort to car camping for my outdoor experiences for the rest of my life. That was assuming I'd actually want any more outdoor experiences beyond day one.

Knowing how low completion rates are and knowing how difficult every step of the trail was for me, I'm still amazed that I actually made it to the end. I started the trail with a dangerous mindset. I thought that the only goal of thru-hiking was to get from point A to point B as quickly as possible, with as little pain as possible. For some, that goal might work, but for me, I quickly learned that my original goal was hardly worthwhile for my physical or mental sanity. I also learned that there is a lot more to gain from the simple act of walking other than skinny legs and golf ball-sized blisters.

There is much more meaning in the goal of living out the experience of getting from start to finish. The important stuff worth remembering is between the mile markers rather than the markers themselves. It took me a long time to realize that the goal of the PCT wasn't just to get to Canada and that the experience meant more than just the chance to burn an amazing amount of calories. Though I will say, that was a fabulous byproduct.

My progression along the trail, both in ability to complete it and ability to enjoy it, started slow and didn't build much in strength or speed until the very end. I'll be the first to say that it was an extremely difficult experience. I had a hard time enjoying the act of walking all day, along with the feelings of being hungry and dirty most of my waking hours. The experience had its shining moments, but there were just as many lows as there were highs to even out the roller coaster of thru-hiking a long-distance trail.

As with most challenging life experiences, they are always better in hindsight. Now that I'm literally out of the trees, I can see the worth of the forest. I can see why an experience such as thru-hiking the PCT has made me who I am, for the better. Now that I've stepped back from the experience, now that both my figurative and literal scars are healed, I can see the worth in such an adventure and the validity in the life lessons that it taught me. It has taken me a long time to be able to fully articulate these lessons.

The life lessons I've described on the upcoming pages are in order of both how I learned them on the trail and how they met my needs, starting out at the most basic and moving on to the more complex. Our most basic needs for water, food, and shelter are those that we tend to fulfill first before moving on to higher-reaching needs that speak to our life's fulfillment and happiness. Many people may never move beyond the most basic needs, just as they may never move beyond learning the most basic lessons in life. Through my life's experience, not only myself, but others, can see that life's far reaching lessons are out there to be learned.

It should also be noted that though I can now fully express these life lessons and how I came to learn them, I still struggle in my daily life to live them out. Just as they are easy to learn, given the right circumstances, they are just as easy to forget, also given the right circumstances. It's easy to go on autopilot when life gets hard and it's easier to toss the lessons to the side than it is to fully live them.

Despite the difficulty I went through to learn these life lessons, as well as the difficulty I go through now to implement them, I'm grateful for every moment on the trail in which I learned them and even more grateful that I have the ability to share them with you. It is my hope that these lessons, exemplified in tales from the trail, speak to some part of your life and make you pause for at least a moment to say, "Hey, it's just like on the trail."

As for the nitty-gritty details on how a thru-hike is completed, the hundreds of pieces involved in building the puzzle of a thru-hike make it nearly impossible to declare that one method is best for everyone. There are the same basic needs for all hikers: water, food, clothing and shelter. Beyond that, the shaping of the thru-hike is solely in each individual hiker's hands. It really is as simple as putting one foot in front of the other or as complicated as months of research and planning.

Optimist and I started the PCT somewhere in the middle of the scale of being fully prepared and totally winging it. We knew walking would be our most important act, so we focused on that from the beginning. Since it was the biggest item on our daily list, everything else was lower on the priority list. Besides buying the gear and packing enough food for a few days at the start, Optimist and I let the trail plan itself. We had neither the time nor the desire to figure out much beyond the basics of the trail, and even those proved to be more difficult than we ever expected.

Because it was a learn-as-you-go experience for us, so it will be for you as you read the ensuing pages. I won't begin to try and explain each part of a long-distance hike, nor would that be enjoyable to read. Instead, just as we did with each step, the way of life will become clearer to you, it will seem manageable at some point, and you just might be overwhelmed with the clarity that comes in seeing a long-distance trail such as the PCT for what it is worth and what it has to offer.

Though an adventure such as this may never be in your scope of desire or ability, the lessons that follow can apply to any walk of life, whether walking is actually involved or not. You don't need to be a hiker to understand how these stories could apply to everyday life. While long-distance hiking is not for everyone, it's mainly because almost no one tries it. I invite you to step into the classroom known as nature and experience at least a teaspoon's worth of the life of a thru-hiker by reading on, even if your only motivation is to find out how a pessimist like me made it to the end with a polar opposite like Optimist.

2 WATER IS GOOD

As part of our planning for the hike, Optimist and I bought one guidebook that covered the entire trail, in addition to receiving guidebooks for different sections of California as a gift from a friend. We didn't purchase guidebooks for Oregon or Washington because we knew Rocketcop was in possession of those, and I doubted my ability to even make it that far. Once Rocketcop knew he was committed to the trail, he emailed us a picture of the books positioned proudly on the back of his toilet. It was the perfect reading material for that space in the home, yet ironically so because that creature comfort was one of the first things to go on the trail. In thinking about sharing guidebooks, I'm amazed that we all assumed that not only would all of us make it as far as Washington, but that we'd also be together to share the books.

The guidebooks we used were a great reference material, full of information on history, animal life, plant life, and even rock life along the trail. They had descriptions of each section, detailed maps, and helpful tips for both thru-hikers and all other types of hikers. I tried reading most of the book on Southern California before departing, but found it hard to read about a world so foreign to me that I couldn't even picture what I'd soon be walking through. I also didn't like the fact that the book started with facts about animals, my main concerns being rattlesnakes, bears, and mountain lions. I was ready to quit the trail before I'd even started once I read the advice on what *not* to do in the presence of a mountain lion: "To flee is to die." That phrase repeated itself in my head many times along the way as my heart raced in response to any rustle in the bushes.

The only problem with some of the guidebooks was that each one weighed about two pounds and took up both precious space and weight in the pack. They simply were not ideal to carry once we started the thru-hike. When each pound matters, as an ideal pack weight is at least under twenty-five pounds, it sounds ridiculous to devote two of them solely to a book. Regardless, we started with one guidebook for the Southern California section (by Schirfin, Schaffer, Winnett and Jenkins), hoping its information and maps would outweigh the cons of its weight.

In contrast to the heavier guidebooks, we also used the *Pacific Crest Trail Data Book*, or the data book as we called it, by Benedict Go. The book covered information for the entire trail and was much lighter, as it was a small, compact book full of bare bones, yet essential information to get oneself from Mexico to Canada. The book listed data points along the way, with data points being something of significance to a hiker, such as water, a road crossing, a town...all the things needed for survival and mental sanity in breaking up the trail into very small chunks. It let us know what to expect, what to look forward to, and how to plan our day. It was essential to our life on the trail.

The data book was broken into the five major sections of the PCT: Southern California, Central California, Northern California, Oregon and Washington. While it showed the mileage between two points, such as a creek and a dirt road, it also showed a running tally of the trail the entire way and the elevation of each data point. For quick and easy reference, there was also a column with a code for each type of data point, such as W for water, G for groceries, and PO for post office. It really was a fabulous book that we probably thumbed through thousands of times over the duration of the trail. One of my favorite camp time traditions was looking through the upcoming pages of the book. I loved to memorize the water availability for the next day, the distance to the next town, and the difficulty of the upcoming climbs. The proof of that tradition now shows itself in the grimy cover and delicate pages as we gingerly sift through it today like it's an artifact of another time.

In reading the guidebook for the Southern California section during our preparations for the trip, one piece of information I took away from it was the lack of water. The authors painted a pretty grim picture of hundreds of miles with very few abundant, reliable water sources. I remember saying to Optimist, "Hey, we should probably think about this before we go." The words dry, hot, and desert struck a chord in me. Addressing the water situation of Southern California seemed like a good thing to do before leaving the well-flowing supply of water from our sinks and showerhead in our Annapolis apartment.

I was hoping the authors of one guidebook were being overly dramatic as they wrote about the trail, so I checked to see what the data book had to say about water. To my dismay, the data book complied with the information in the guidebook. The first two pages actually didn't look that bad, as I counted twelve points along the way that claimed to have water in the first forty-one miles. Then I flipped the page and learned the term, "Water Alert." These two words were typed in bold, black letters on the page, with a measurement of miles next to the words. I flipped the page again and saw even more water alerts with even bigger measurements of miles. I again said to Optimist as I flipped through the pages, still in our cozy apartment, "We *really* should pay attention to this."

In the data book, a water alert is a section of twelve miles or more, often *way* more, without any water on the trail or within a half mile of it. In the Southern California section alone, a 702.8 mile section, there were fifteen water alerts. Our first water alert lasted almost twenty-five miles, with the longest being over thirty-five miles. Upon finishing each water alert section, after finally reaching the long sought after water source, I often felt like we crossed the finish line of a marathon, a marathon in which we weren't provided with water or electrolytes. Imagine if marathons today did not provide tables of water to its participants every few miles. The already small percentage of marathoners in the world would no doubt shrink considerably. Now put that marathon distance on the trail, 26.2 miles, again without providing water, and you have what is an example of a water alert along the PCT. It starts to seem a little crazy to willingly put oneself in such a situation.

It took us thirty-two days to walk the Southern California section. We had a water alert a little more than every two days. Just to be cruel, so it seemed, one water alert took place as we literally walked on the pavement covering the Los Angeles aqueduct, the water supply for most of the people of LA. We imagined drinking the water as we pressed our ears to the pavement. It sounded like a tunnel full of crystal clear, rushing, plentiful snow melt from the Sierra Nevada. We ached for the chance to find a hole in the pavement and said to ourselves, "If only we could dip our bottles in for at least a sip of the thirst-quenching liquid."

All of this amounts to the fact that we had water on our brains at all times, the entire trail. Though Southern California was especially guilty of causing such a side effect, it lasted all the way until Canada. It wasn't until I took a sip from the water fountain in the Seattle airport that I knew I no longer had to worry about water.

There was not one day on the trail where water wasn't on my mind. Gathering enough water to drink and to cook with was a constant to-do on my daily check list, right along with eat, sleep and walk. I needed enough water to keep me hydrated and enough water to cook lunch and dinner. Walking induced quite a bit of sweating and sweating induced quite a bit of thirst. The recommendation of eight glasses of water a day did not apply to us. I consumed at least a gallon of water each day and I could still feel a trace of cottonmouth nearly every day. Since most of our meals were dehydrated and required water in order to be cooked, meal time also meant a need for water to boil noodles or rehydrate beans.

I thought about water all the time. I thought about it when I woke to the morning sun climbing its daily ladder in the sky and I often woke up feeling like a sponge that was left sitting out overnight on the kitchen counter, dry and ready to soak up water. I thought about water when I pulled out the data book each day, scanning ahead twenty to thirty miles to see if we could plan our next night's camp near a water source. If we weren't camping next to water, we would stock up on water at our last water source for the day before heading to a dry camping spot. Not only did I have to account for water to drink for the rest of the day, I also had to think about water for dinner, for breakfast the next morning, and for the miles the next day before reaching the next water source. Because of all this planning, we tried our best to camp near water each night, but it just wasn't possible each evening.

When we could plan our day to camp near water, it meant less weight to carry during the afternoon and evening miles. As you'll learn later, the less weight carried around in the pack, the better, especially since each liter of water weighs around two pounds. Do the math, taking into account that I consumed at least four liters of water a day, and that's not counting water used for cooking. The numbers are humbling, weighing in at eight pounds of water alone that I drank a day, on top of all my other pack weight. Thus, the less water I had to carry over long distances, the happier I was.

Water sources could be streams, creeks, lakes, rivers, or even a trickle from a crevice in the rock. Our ears became accustomed to listening for that unmistakable sound of the flow of water, bubbling up from a spring or cascading over rocks. When we did come across water sources, we questioned whether we should fill up completely at a good-looking water source or just try and make it to the next one. It's like filling up completely at a gas station and spending the forty bucks on a tank where the gas is a decent price, or just putting in five bucks for now and hoping to find a better price down the road. Only we weren't weighing the cost, but rather the actual weight.

It was a dangerous decision to make. It was hard to know if the next water source would be dry or unable to be purified, or if we should enjoy the lesser pack weight of water that we only needed at that moment. Because these decisions were often laid before us, water was a stressful part of the trail that I was glad to be rid of when I re-entered society. I rejoiced in the moment when I could simply turn on a faucet to receive endless gallons of a substance that managed to set up shop and occupy my thoughts for months.

Amazingly, despite carrying eight pounds of water at a time in Southern California, and nearly that much for the rest of the trail, we were considered risk-takers by other hikers. Some carried two gallons of water at a time, adding up to a back-breaking sixteen pounds of water. That's in addition to anything else occupying precious pack space and weight. I couldn't and still cannot fathom carrying more than eight pounds of water. Rather than carry more water, we often drank until it hurt when we arrived at a water source. We would polish off at least an entire liter of water before leaving the source for good so that our thirst wouldn't hit us until much later down the trail. The tactic worked well, but my thirst always seemed to reach me sooner than expected.

Despite my preparation in reading about water availability along the trail and despite my warnings to Optimist that we really should prepare for this part of the trail, the lack of water was still a stunning realization to be hit with so early on in the trail. We were completely dependent on this natural resource over which we had no control and there wasn't much of it going around. Hello Mother Nature, goodbye kitchen sink.

I learned about the goodness of water on the very first day of the PCT. I started the trail at 11:00 a.m. on Tuesday, May 16, 2007, accompanied by Optimist, Rocketcop and Animal. Optimist had hiked the Appalachian Trail with both of them in 2000, so it was fitting that they joined us on the PCT.

Optimist met Animal as a freshman in college and they became even better friends when they hiked the AT together after deciding to leave college, as the school no longer appealed to either of them. Animal is the type that can be so focused on the task at hand that there is no stopping him, yet at other times can be so wildly free-spirited and off the beaten path that he nears self-destruction. We hoped he was in the former mode when we started the PCT. Rocketcop, who earned his trail name after singing his own version of *Rocky Top* at a bar with a karaoke machine, is as equally positive as Optimist, but with a thick New Jersey accent and a knack for making most situations laughable. Them, along with Optimist, were some of the best people I could have surrounded myself with at the start of such a journey. I knew I could stay focused as long as Animal did, I could laugh with Rocketcop's lighthearted personality, and I could be supported by Optimist.

We started close to the heat of the day, as we just couldn't seem to get going that morning in order to leave San Diego. It was quite a feat to coordinate four people's arrival into San Diego and to get a ride to Campo, the starting point of the trail. The drive isn't exactly a short hop from the city, but rather at least an hour's worth of driving through traffic and later on dirt roads. In the end, we made it to the start that first day and that was all that mattered.

Since we started so late and since it was our first day of hiking, we knew we didn't want to walk very far. We all agreed to get to mile marker sixteen, Hauser Creek, which the data book noted was a winter and early spring creek. We figured the trail gods were on our side and that we'd still have a bubbling creek awaiting our first day's camp. We didn't factor in the possibility that "seasonally dry" in the Southern California portion of the data book really meant, "Don't ever count on this water source, as it's most likely so dried out that you wonder if there is ever really a season when it has water." It's a bit wordy, but for our purposes, it was how I came to describe that first water source.

Getting to the creek with enough water wasn't a problem. We all started with two liters each of liquids and had conserved them all day despite a dusty, hot beginning to the trail. Looking back, we probably should have started with four liters each of some sort of liquid, whether it was water or a sports drink like Gatorade. But, we had the "learn as you go" mentality, and though we all arrived to Hauser Creek with at least some liquid left, only Rocketcop had plain water. Getting to the creek with enough water for cooking dinner, for drinking in the evening, and for drinking the next morning was a completely different scenario that we weren't prepared for. The sparse amount of water that Rocketcop had left was not nearly enough for all of us for the evening, nor would we have asked him to sacrifice it for the group.

It was about six in the evening when we made it to Hauser Creek. The only sign of it being a creek was that the creek ground sat slightly lower than the trail. Its bed was covered in dried up, thirsty leaves and was slightly shaded from the trees that hung over it from the banks of the creek. The word that best describes the scene is brown. The ground, the leaves, and the trees were all a shade of brown, without any hope of reaching a hint of green due to the lack of water.

Our ankles already matched the scenery, as the dust from the dry trail had painted them brown as well. When we walked in the creek to survey its lack of water, the parched leaves crunched and crackled under our feet. There was no visible sign of life. It seemed to lie still, unable to move because of the stiffness caused from such a long drought of water. I'm quite sure I would have passed it had Rocketcop not been there to recognize it as our mile marker.

There we were, Rocketcop, Optimist and I, with just a few swigs of water and Gatorade left among the three of us. Animal was behind as that point, as he carried a considerably heavier pack. Knowing he was probably the least prepared out of all of us, we guessed that he didn't have enough water to camp with for the evening. As we stood there looking at each other in disbelief, I pulled out the data book and checked the next mile marker that had a w (for water) marked next to it. Standing there at the dry creek, which also had a w marked next to it, taught me early on that counting on the w was not such a great idea. Though it was our own faulty preparations that got us in that situation, it was still hard to swallow the choices we had left ourselves. I thought to myself, as I scanned the next few miles in the data book, desperately hoping we wouldn't have to walk much more, "What did I get myself into?"

I saw that about four and a half miles up the trail was the Lake Morena Campground. It had piped water, a true luxury that we learned was few and far between. Most importantly, it was an honest water source. Unfortunately, we didn't have any other choice but to keep walking to reach more water. It was a choice that was often the case when a wrench was thrown into the plans. All three of us made the decision without Animal that we were moving on.

Before leaving Hauser Creek, we pooled our water together to leave Animal a half a bottle of water. We placed it on top of a small note, a torn off corner of loose paper in Optimist's pack, and set it in the middle of the trail so Animal would trip on it if he missed it. We told him where we'd be for the night and hoped he had enough energy to follow us. It seemed strange and a bit eerie to already be forced to make a plan B on day one. It was also an omen for a sub-lesson that rings true in almost all the life lessons learned on the trail. We can't control everything.

The worst part about the extra miles wasn't the distance, it wasn't that my pack was heavy, and it wasn't that I was tired and just wanted to stop moving. It was that the first mile and a half of the extra miles was a steep uphill that literally stared us in the face. It towered above us as we stood at the banks of the dry creek and contemplated our water situation for the night.

After much heavy breathing and internal whining (ok, a little external whining as well from me), we made it to the top of the climb. As I exhaled a sigh of relief upon reaching the top, I heard Rocketcop exclaim, "Whoa, Sally!"

His sudden yelp startled me and I snapped my head up to see what he was so excited about. I saw that he was looking just to the side of my right calf and I jumped in my skin and felt my whole body tingle. I expected to turn and see a rattlesnake behind me, coiled and ready to strike as I swung around to face it. Instead I saw the most beautiful sight. Tucked next to a boulder were two gallon jugs of water labeled, "For thru-hikers."

It was glorious and I immediately realized just how good water was on the trail. It was also the moment I realized that other people cared so selflessly about our well being out there on the trail that they had hiked up to that point just to drop off the water. It was downhill either way on the trail, so someone had hiked uphill just to leave water for hikers they'd most likely never meet.

All three of us filled our bottles about halfway and immediately chugged the contents. It was a warm, tea-like temperature from sitting outside in the heat for who knows how long, but still intensely satisfying and we drank it quickly. There was a hint of plastic to its flavor, but I didn't care. I nearly kissed the jug itself and would have

kissed the person who left it there had t‍
After a few minutes of celebration for the
on the trail, we filled our bottles halfway on‍
hike. We didn't fill them fully since we knew o‍
be walking behind us, having their dreams fulfill‍
sight of the gallon jugs of liquid life. After that we
downhill to the campground, getting in just as dusk‍
requiring the need for headlamps upon arrival. We d‍
hearts' content from the piped water in the campgroun‍
fully appreciative of water, our true life-line on the trail.

Day one certainly wasn't the last time we were burned by a‍
water along the trail. Though we became accustomed to carry‍
heavy load of water during most of the dry sections, there we‍
moments where, just like day one, we simply had to keep walking to
reach water. It was at least an easy decision to make and it always
meant more miles were accomplished, but it wasn't the most enjoyable
part of the trail. It was the most basic, tangible lesson that showed up
early and stayed consistent the entire way.

Another part of the water worries, apart from the availability of it
on the trail, was how it was made drinkable. Though most water
sources looked like enticing, crystal clear, harmless cascades of water
flowing downstream, it was safe to assume they contained some sort of
unfriendly microscopic organism. Two names we learned early on the
trail were giardia and cryptosporidium. Though we couldn't spell them
or even pronounce them correctly, we knew they were two parts of the
trail to avoid at all costs. They're both infection-inducing organisms
that are not only uncomfortable to experience, through the likes of
abdominal cramps, nausea, and diarrhea, but also require medicine to
cure their ailments. Also known as, feeling like crap and getting off the
trail to see a doctor…two actions to avoid.

There were few faucets, if any, sticking out of the side of the
mountain, ready and available to disperse clean, bacteria-free water.
Even if there were such faucets, I still wouldn't have trusted the purity
of the water. Most of the water we encountered needed some sort of
purification treatment in order to make it safe to drink. Whether it was
a small stream, a creek or a lake, it was safe to assume that the water
should be purified. Many organisms, including plants, humans and
animals, rely on water sources and build homes around those water
sources. If an animal has set up a home near that water source, as

d in the mounds of poop on or near the side of the trail, it's
at some trace of that poop has made its way into the adjacent
source. Thus, upon reaching a water source, I always envisioned
sort of animal's poop nearby, contaminating the water and
ving no chances to be taken.

As you can imagine, there's more than one way to purify water.
cause of that, differing water purification methods were a hot topic
mong thru-hikers along the trail. This was especially evident in the
beginning when we were all fine-tuning the different aspects of hiking.

Out of all the methods out there, including but not limited to a
water filter, chemical treatments, ultraviolet light treatments…we
started with a water pump. It was considered an old school method
compared to others that were lighter in weight or newer in technology.
Rocketcop also started out with a pump, while others we met used
some sort of chemical or tablet. The pump's upside was that it pumped
a half a gallon of water in just a few effortless minutes. While others
had to wait up to a half hour to drink their water after the chemical
treatments did their thing, we could pump a bottle of water, drink it,
and then fill it up again before the others could even dream of a sip of
water. Other hikers were certainly covetous of our water pump early
on.

The downside was that it weighed around two pounds, and
Optimist and I each started out with our own. We quickly realized that
carrying two water pumps was excessive weight in our packs. We gave
one of them to Optimist's brother, Jeff, when he met us in a town
several days into the trail. The plan was for him to mail us the unused
pump about halfway through the hike.

At first, one pump sufficed for both of us and we could lessen our
joint pack weight by two pounds. The pump worked great when the
water source was clear of any debris, dirt, or general muckiness.
However, once we had to downgrade to the less desirable water
sources because of sheer necessity, it had a hard time keeping up. Thus,
the other big downside to a water pump reared its ugly head just a
couple of weeks after we resorted to one pump. With just a few
sketchy water sources full of dirt and debris, its filter was clogged to
the point of being useless. Those few effortless minutes of pumping
turned into at least five minutes of an all-out upper body workout to
pump even one bottle's worth of water, and we had to fill up eight
bottles at a time.

We noticed the pump slowing down just before we made it to the town of Kennedy Meadows, around seven hundred miles into the trail. The town is the beginning of Central California, a section which is known to have the most abundant, high quality water on the trail. The highlight of our time spent at the Kennedy Meadows General Store, an establishment seemingly in the middle of nowhere, was our mini reunion with Jeff, Optimist's brother. He drove the few hours from Los Angeles to spend his Saturday afternoon visiting with us and reminiscing about the trail thus far. He still had our second, nearly unused water pump, at his apartment. He offered to bring it out to us along with a box of food for the next leg of the journey, but we made a rather hasty decision for him to leave it at his apartment, convinced that our water pump should last until halfway up the trail, which was another six hundred miles.

Entering Central California was like flipping a switch. The scenery changed from mostly brown to lots of greens. There were trees that offered shade, the temperatures cooled in the evenings with higher elevations, and it didn't seem quite so hot in the day. The data book was also lined with frequent water sources.

Despite the beautiful scenery, our first evening in Central California wasn't exactly what we expected. We stayed at Cow Creek and we immediately knew why it was named as such. It was littered with cows grazing along the banks of the well flowing, fifteen-foot wide creek, as well as their cow paddies (poop), sprinkling the grassy meadow butting right up against the creek. It was difficult to walk, let alone find a campsite, among the meadow's rutted, poop-laden ground. There was no doubt in our minds that the water had to be purified. For the first time along the trail, I was both scared and repulsed to drink the first few swigs of water, knowing what kind of organisms could be in there had the water pump not fully done its job. I still shudder at the thought of drinking that water while I sat there surrounded by cow poop seeping into such a seemingly good water source.

Cow Creek was hard on our water pump. I'm sure it had to work hard to get all that crap, literally, out of the water. The next day wasn't very forgiving either. Though there were quite a few water sources in the data book, several of them ended up being lightly flowing, really dirty, or at least a quarter mile off the trail. The Central California land of freely flowing, crystal clear water sources that had been promised to us during the first seven hundred miles was non-existent, at least in the first few days of that section. We paid dearly for believing that promise.

After eleven miles into the next day's hike, the day after the Cow Creek experience, we'd only come across one decent water source. It was more of a trickle than a flow and was very shallow, so we had a difficult time filling up our bottles. The other downside to a water pump is that there needs to be about a two-inch deep pool of water, preferably much deeper, in which to dip the filter. It cannot simply sit on a trickle of water and be expected to grab enough water in the filter to generate a good pump's worth of water. After moving on from the trickling stream, we also passed another creek that was barely more than a patch of wet ground that we had to hop over. We should have known that our next water source, Death Canyon Creek, did not have a good ring to its name. Who puts death in the same name with creek?

The creek consisted of pools of thick, orange liquid that stunk of rotten, dead fish.

Unfortunately, it was the death of our water pump. We walked up and down its banks to find the best looking pool of stagnant water and opted for the least orange-tinted one that was void of anything dead floating in it. We filled up a couple of bottles and rather than pump the water right there at the source, which was a few minutes' walk down a side trail, we took the bottles back to the main trail. Next to the trail was a large tree with loosely hanging branches that were swaying in the afternoon's warm breeze. Under the tree was a cool patch of dirt, perfect for pumping water and eating a snack. We got to work on pumping the water from the contaminated bottles to the clean bottles while we snacked on candy bars and crackers.

At that point the pump was at least a really great arm workout. We had to stand over the pump, putting most of our body weight on the handle in order to push it down. It's not a good thing when the water pump is a workout. It's supposed to be easy, quick, and almost fun to pump out a gallon of water. It had definitely lost its element of fun.

Optimist had pumped about a half a bottle, around sixteen ounces, when the pump literally exploded in his hands. Parts flew out across the dirt, water spewed everywhere, and Optimist and I stood there bewildered. I was stopped in my tracks as I raised my Snickers bar to my mouth, sustaining it in midair as my eyes met Optimist's. We were in shock and disbelief at the sight of our broken water pump. Before completely losing our composure, we tried fixing it, putting all the pieces back together where they seemed to fit. Once again, it blew out on us after just a couple of pumps. It was hopeless. Our pump was broken and we had no other alternatives with which to purify water.

As Optimist and I stood there with our water pump in pieces on the ground, both our minds worked towards a solution. We at least had two things going for us at the time. One, we were with Rocketcop and Out of Order, other hikers that had been around us for the last few days. Out of Order knew what it was like for things to go wrong. He had started the trail on borrowed gear because the airline he flew with to the start of the trail lost his baggage and therefore everything he needed to hike. Our water pump breaking was just a small hiccup compared to his trail beginnings, which fittingly so, were out of order.

Rocketcop and Out of Order selflessly stepped up and helped us get water with their water purifiers. Rocketcop had been smart in placing a bandanna over his water pump's filter so that debris and dirt were not as debilitating to his pump as they were to ours. Out of Order used a purification system that when placed in a bottle of water, emitted an ultraviolet light that from seemingly sheer magic, purified the water. Since we were already comfortable with a water pump, we opted for water from Rocketcop's pump.

The only downside to our backup water plan was that Rocketcop and Out of Order could not be with us forever. It was too much to ask of them to use their water purification systems indefinitely, nor did we even contemplate that option. We simply knew that our plan of using Rocketcop's and Out of Order's purification systems would be about as short-lived as the life of our water pump.

The second factor in our favor was that we were in Central California. Though the first miles of the section proved to be difficult for water availability, we knew it would get better. Awaiting us in the section were high elevations and snow melt. Fewer animals were living at the higher elevations above tree line, where there weren't plants to eat or trees to live near. Higher elevation presented loose rocks and gray-colored scenery in contrast to deep blue skies and lots of snow. Lots of snow and an oncoming summer heat in mid-June meant snow melt and quickly flowing water sources. We would soon literally see the highest points in the landscape because we were so physically close to them and we could see the exact snow melt that supplied the clear streams we were crossing. Thus, our next method of water purification was hatched. We chose to drink straight from the sources.

We'd heard of other hikers doing the entire trail without any water purifications systems even from day one, so we tried it out ourselves. At that point, we really didn't have a choice until we made it to a town.

From that point on, until reaching Truckee, California, over eleven hundred miles into the trail, we did not purify our water. We relied solely on the water sources that we felt were safe enough to drink without any kind of purification. We were smart about drinking from upstream, from water flowing swiftly at higher elevations, and avoided lakes and other standing water. Amazingly, we never got sick or even felt the trace of a stomach ache. In addition, the quality of the water straight from the snowmelt and the fresh water springs was unmatched to any water I'd ever tasted. I used to think people were crazy for describing a taste to water. How can something clear have a taste? It can, it did, and it was wonderful. The crisp, core-shaking coldness of the water as it traveled from our mouths to our stomachs, with no trace of flavor other than just plain clean, satisfied the hard work it took to hike to the highest of elevations.

Once we arrived in Truckee, California, near Lake Tahoe, we stopped pressing our luck and started using bleach as our new water purification system. We'd received advice from other thru-hikers that used bleach and decided to try it. We picked up eye droppers and used empty, travel-size shampoo bottles for the bleach, so not only was it a new way to purify water, but it also weighed just ounces compared to our original pumps that weighed pounds. Again, we never had so much as the trace of a stomach ache along the trail. I think that luck played a small role in that as well, as I don't dare claim any sort of genius on our part. I know better than that.

Water is one of our most basic needs, yet it's something that most of us never give a second thought to. How many times do you ask yourself during the day, "Where am I going to get my next bottle of water from?" If anything, I ask myself this question because I have to choose between two kitchens at the office, not because I question whether the next creek I cross will be flowing or not.

Now that I live a normal life again, where I get my water from a faucet with the turn of a wrist and a knob, I like to think that I still fully appreciate water and all its clean, clear goodness. I'm sure I waste a few more drops than I would have allowed myself to use on the trail, but I'm fully aware of my water consumption now that I know how hard it is not only to ration it, but also to be void of it.

Even after having been finished with the trail for years now, it's still a little strange to me just how accessible water is to me in my daily life. I'm surrounded by opportunities to drink purified water nearly effortlessly, whether buying it in a store or having it delivered to me in my home via my kitchen sink. It took me a long time after the trail to get used to turning on the sink for water. I'd literally giggle out loud at the fascination of turning the knob and seeing clean, clear water pour out.

To this day, I think to myself, "Does anyone else realize how amazing this is?"

That amazement doesn't even take into account that not only can we purify it before it comes out in endless amounts, but we can also control its temperature. Simply astounding.

Something else that stayed with me is my water evaluation hat. Every time we are driving, running or walking, and I see a creek, a lake, or some water source, I evaluate it as if it is a knee-jerk reaction to water. I look at the water flow, the depth, what is surrounding it, like roads or paths, how high in elevation it is…I can't stop my brain from calculating the quality of the water. I think to myself, "Oh, that's a great water source, I'd totally drink from that," or "Whoa, stay away from that creek, I bet it has all kinds of runoff from the road."

I became so accustomed to looking at every single source of water for over three months, that it's hard to turn off that side of my brain. It wasn't a lingering effect I was prepared for, but it is fun to see that this "skill" has stuck with me well after finishing the trail.

Water is good. It's a simple, yet important lesson for anyone to learn. Unfortunately, it's most easily learned when water is in restricted quantities or less than desirable quality. It's hard to conserve water or fully appreciate it when it's so easy to access from our own faucets. Though I can turn on my faucet just as easily as the next person, I like to think that I take a little pause before I do so, thanking whoever organized this system of such accessible, clean water, and reminding myself that water is oh so good.

3 BUT FOOD IS BETTER

Years before I had even a pinch of a thought of hiking the PCT, I went on a ten-mile hike in the Shenandoah National Park with Optimist, on a portion of the Appalachian Trail. It was a cloudy, misty day in late June, and I was cold during most of the hike. I wore a tank top and running shorts and was constantly fighting off goose bumps. The trees felt like they were bearing down on me as we made our way down the trail, offering little views beyond the expanse of thickly wooded green in front of me.

I mainly looked forward to the end of the hike. I wanted my creature comforts of food, shelter and warmth. I also awaited the chocolate chip cookies that we'd packed for lunch earlier that morning and that had a home in Optimist's backpack.

Up until that point, I'd spent very little time on a trail. To add to my paltry camping experience, my hiking experience thus far had been walking the connections of trails from my backyard to my friends' houses back in the fifth grade. I'm not even sure they qualified as trails. Most were worn paths through strangers' back yards and stretches down subdivisions' blacktop roads.

That particular day, it was Optimist's idea to go for a hike on the AT. I thought I'd at least give it a try. It definitely wasn't my thing, before or after the day's hike.

About halfway through the hike, we ran into a hiker going the opposite way, as we were going south on the trail. He looked much dirtier, scruffier, and simply more worn than us. He had obviously been out there for more than just a day or two. Even my virgin trail eyes

25

could tell he was a different kind of hiker. His shirt looked like it had been white at some point in its life, with no hope of ever going back again. There wasn't much pep in his step. It had been replaced with a semi-shuffling march, and his dirty legs and heavy boots lumbered along with the rest of his body. Most of all, he desperately needed a shave. Thankfully, I kept my distance, so scents are not in my recollection.

Optimist, having thru-hiked the AT just a few years earlier, excitedly asked the hiker, "Are you a thru-hiker?"

As a broad smile came across the man's face, his beard seemingly littered with crumbs of past meals and the crow's feet around his eyes filled with dirt, he proudly answered, "Yes I am."

At once, the two started talking about the trail like long-lost souls finally brought together again. My presence was not acknowledged by either of them.

Honestly, I was a bit annoyed. I didn't give a hoot who this stranger was, as the term thru-hiker didn't do much for me at that point. The sooner we could finish the hike, the sooner we could eat the lunch we had packed and get back into our car, a better mode of transportation and source of warmth.

I quickly lost interest as I realized I had nothing to add to the conversation. I'd had enough of the outsider's circle, so I started to walk further down the trail, knowing Optimist would eventually catch up. I hoped that my exit would signal him to wrap it up.

After three steps down the trail, I stopped mid-stride when I heard Optimist ask the hiker, "Do you need any food?"

"Oh, hell no! He is not giving away our lunch!" I thought to myself.

I turned and stared at him in disbelief as he casually offered up all our food. He graciously opened his backpack and emptied the much-anticipated contents of potato salad, cheese sandwiches, pretzel sticks, apples and chocolate chip cookies. I was so heated and speechless that I stormed off, furious that he was willing to make us go hungry just so he could appease this stranger. Most of all, I couldn't believe he didn't even ask me if I cared that he gave up our entire lunch.

When he caught me later down the trail, I was still fuming. My feet pounded the ground with each stride. I hoped to take my anger out on the earth beneath me. He was trotting at that point, light as the air under his feet, floating in his good deed.

"Why did you have to give away all our food?" I gruffly asked, restraining myself from yelling at him. I knew whatever answer he gave would push me further over the edge.

"Julie, you don't understand. He's a thru-hiker; he's always hungry! I remember when I was out here, and even if I was carrying food, I always took food if people offered it. I could always eat more. It's not like we can't just go get more food; we have a car. He's just walking. It's my way of giving back. It's the least I can do for another thru-hiker." He pleaded with me to understand the unspoken ways of the woods and I was having none of it.

I wanted to say that the hiker looked perfectly capable of walking to get his own food rather than taking ours, but I didn't. I saw that no amount of complaining on my end would make Optimist feel guilty for my hunger pangs. I simply trudged on, keeping my words to a minimum. They were all negative, so it would do no good for them to be spoken.

I still didn't understand even hours after I'd filled my belly, after the hunger wasn't adding fuel to my anger, why Optimist had given our food away to a complete stranger just because he was walking on a trail. No amount of explaining would make me understand it. Only being a thru-hiker myself would teach me that lesson.

Contrary to popular belief, or at least to frequently asked questions, one does not carry all the food for the entire trail on one's back from Mexico to Canada. Imagine trying to carry, or even plan, four to five months worth of food. It simply cannot be done, nor would one want to hike that way.

Yet, one man came close.

According to the Pacific Crest Trail Association, in 1970, Eric Ryback, popularly known as the first thru-hiker of the PCT, carried an eighty-pound pack. It is said that he only stocked up on food five times during the length of the trip and was loaded with forty pounds of food each time he refilled his pack. Even with that much food, he often ran out of food and foraged or went hungry.

That was enough evidence to convince me that we would stop for food quite a bit. I did not aspire to rival his feats.

Two questions that we field time and again from people are, "How do hikers get food while out in the middle of nowhere," and "What the heck do they eat?" The simple answers are, "Resupplies," and "A lot, but never enough."

One piece of the thru-hiking puzzle is the all important resupply. Resupply becomes one of the most important words to a hiker's trail vocabulary. It refers to the stop in town to stock up on more food from post offices, grocery stores and restaurants in order to make it to the next town.

Thru-hikers obtain food just the way normal citizens do, by stepping inside a store, loading up a shopping cart, and politely paying. The only catch is that stores aren't exactly lining the trail, nor can a midnight craving for cookie dough ice cream be satisfied as easily as a hop in the car and a quick drive to the twenty-four hour Wal-Mart.

A town that offers a means of purchasing food, whether it is a gas station mini-mart, a small general store, or the preferred super-size store, can be as close as a few feet from the trail, or as far as the hiker wishes to walk (or hitchhike). There are quite a few opportunities to stop in towns along the way, to the point where a hiker can buy food as often as every few days, or skip towns and stock up less frequently. The disadvantage of skipping towns, as Eric Ryback would surely agree, is that fewer stops mean a heavier pack. A heavier pack makes hiking all the more difficult, especially on an uphill.

If there is a grocery store in a town or at least some means of purchasing food, there's also most likely a restaurant. Any restaurant will suffice to entice a hiker. A common site is thru-hikers setting up shop in the local restaurants and fitting as much food as possible into their stomachs for the time they are in town. A lot of food fantasizing goes through hikers' minds while out on the trail, so when they actually make those dreams a reality by reaching a town, the food party begins.

In addition to stores and restaurants in towns, there are also post offices. One of the most common methods for thru-hikers to obtain food is by sending it to themselves through the US Postal Service. It's a little known use of post offices, but hikers usually send mail addressed to themselves, even big heavy boxes full of non-perishable food, via general delivery to the post offices lining the trail. Granted, the mail has to be picked up in a reasonable amount of time. I imagine that by the end of the season, the post offices end up with a fairly high number of abandoned boxes.

Months before the hike has even begun, many dreamy-eyed thru-hikers can be found sitting crossed-legged on their living room floor, surrounded by carefully organized piles of non-perishable food items like pasta noodles, nuts, candy bars and dried fruit, all neatly packed in plastic bags, ready to be packed in boxes and shipped to a town they've never heard of. At the same time, the hiker is most likely instructing a close family member on when to mail such boxes so they can time the box's arrival with the hiker's arrival in each town. Luckily, the mailmen up and down the trail are quite used to the thru-hiker community using this system of mailing boxes. They're even friendly upon hoisting the heavy boxes up to the counter so that the hiker can once again carry on up the trail.

In preparing for the hike, we gave friends and family a list of six post offices along the trail that were within a mile's walk of the trail. We suggested that if they wanted to send us anything along the way, such as food, letters, cards…we would gladly accept whatever weight it added to our packs. Because of this list, the US Postal Service made eating along the trail that much more possible. It turned out to be a great way to get luxury items from our moms and grandmothers, such as homemade trail mixes and breads, chocolate covered espresso beans, and flavored drink mixes. It was the best support our family and friends could give us along the way, as food was the way to our hearts.

Most hikers do a combination of all of the above in order to obtain food. The usual routine upon reaching a town is to first quench any thirst or hunger at a restaurant, then pick up any packages at the post office, and finally shop for any supplemental items in the local store. Like water, food is an important part of the trail that is not only necessary for survival, but can also make or break the trail experience. Dealing with constant hunger will drive a hiker both physically and mentally into the ground, yet stops in town for milkshakes, pizza and other town fare are often the best reward for making it through tough miles.

When it comes to what is actually purchased at a store or packed in a box, a hiker will eat whatever they are willing to carry. This can change dramatically over time. There is more to consider than just preferences towards food, as one has to consider the thousands of calories that are burned with each day's mileage. Optimist and I walked an average of nearly twenty-five miles a day, easily burning over five thousand calories a day. The phrase "low calorie" was not in our vocabulary.

The goal is usually to have the most calorically dense, lightest weight and fastest cooking items in the pack. It's a tall order to ask that food replace the thousands of calories burned over the course of the day, that it weigh very little, and that it cook quickly. Peanut butter often makes its way to the top of the list, and I fully partook in eating it by the spoonful. While some hikers eat cold food, meaning they don't cook anything, most hikers use some form of a stove for warm food. Each hiker has some sort of method to cook items like noodles, pasta or rice, and the faster those items cook, the less stove fuel it takes. Less stove fuel means less weight in the pack and less time and energy that have to be spent on filling up on fuel. At first it seems strange to be so focused on pack weight when considering what food to carry, but as the miles start wearing on dead legs burdened under a heavy pack, pack weight is all a hiker can think about. In addition to water and hunger, of course. It's a fine balancing act of food, water and pack weight that constantly shifts between the front and back burners of a thru-hiker's mind.

At first, just like water, it seemed like an insurmountable task for Optimist and me to plan out meals for months of living outside. Food can be an extremely stressful part of the trail if a hiker doesn't learn how to plan out their meals. Running out of food is downright debilitating, but carrying extra days of food is simply stupid. Extra days of food mean extra pack weight and no hiker ever wants extra poundage when arriving in town. There was no point in carrying it from one town to the next; it was just dead weight. Luckily, it became second nature for us prepare for each leg of food from town to town.

Optimist and I spent the two days leading up to the start of the trail with Animal's family in Columbus, Ohio. His brother was employed at the local grocery store and took us shopping for our first few days of trail food. We even got a ten percent discount.

We bought food that Optimist remembered eating on the Appalachian Trail: quick-cooking rice and noodle packages, ramen noodles, dried fruit, Snickers candy bars, M&Ms, and boxed macaroni and cheese. I had no idea what I was getting into. I let him steer the cart, grabbing items off the shelf that I had never bought in my life. As he chose them, I was excited to start eating them. I knew these were items that I would never allow myself to eat in normal circumstances, but that I would definitely allow if I were walking for ten hours each day.

One part of our food preparation that I do wish we had thought through was to ask ourselves what kind of food we might crave in a hot, dry, desert environment. I had thought about how those words affected our water cravings, but not our food ones. If I had thought it through, I may have found that copious amounts of chocolate bars and sweets would not be at the top of the list. That mistake surfaced quickly once the hike started.

On the first day of the hike, when we sat down for our first snack break after a few hot, sun-soaked miles, the only food I could see was chocolate. It looked and sounded awful. It looked awful because all the M&Ms had melted in their bag and all my Snickers bars had melted in their wrappers, creating warm, squishy tubes. The salty meals we had packed, the noodle and rice packages, were strictly reserved for dinner. They required cooking and cooking was reserved for camp time when the hiking was finished for the day. I was left with melted chocolate and dried fruit for my snacks. I went hungry instead and stuck to my liquids.

By the second day, in addition to hunger, since I refused to subsist on my chocolate snacks in the stifling heat of Southern California, I had a small bout of heat stroke. My head pounded with every step I took, my body felt cold on the inside despite being encased in heat, and my stomach revolted the second evening when we set up camp at the Burnt Rancheria Campground. I could only eat a bite of the cheddar broccoli rice dinner. It was the salty meal that I craved so badly, but I had to forfeit it to Optimist. He was concerned that I couldn't eat, but secretly rejoiced in eating two packages of food.

On the morning of the third day, we hiked a few miles to our first resupply, the Mt. Laguna General Store, a small store and post office. Once there we wasted no time in finding the salty stuff, stocking up on chips, peanuts, and crackers. I sat on the store's front steps with Optimist and Rocketcop in the early morning, reveling in my new-found love of salty food, my key to making it through the desert.

After day three, our trail diet rarely ventured beyond the typical fare of packaged rice and noodle meals, candy bars, peanuts and generally processed food. Though we managed to choose foods with a high caloric content, they didn't necessarily equate to quality energy that lasted for very long. They never seemed to be able to satisfy our energy needs.

Considering our small amount of preparation before the trail, our food choices worked well for at least the first seven hundred miles, or about four and a half weeks, through Southern California. I was quite happy to start my days with a King Size Snickers bar. There may not be another time in my life that I can do that and still lose weight. But, just after Kennedy Meadows, the entrance to the Sierra Mountains and Central California, we realized that carrying lower quality food wasn't cutting it in the harder, higher climbs and cooler temperatures. The processed food that fueled us through the desert just wasn't enough energy anymore and we learned it the hard way.

We left Kennedy Meadows with ten days of food, increasing our pack weight well into the high forty and low fifty pounds range. I've often heard that a pack should not weigh more than a quarter to a third of a person's body weight. I weighed under a hundred and twenty pounds at that point and Optimist was under a hundred and thirty. It was probably a bit much for our frames.

Optimist and I had carried ten days' worth of food twice before that section, so we felt adequately prepared in how much food we'd need to sustain us. It was an amount that we had been "satisfied" with before. "Satisfied," because we could always eat more, but we still ate enough calories to hike our miles.

We realized by Pinchot Pass, around eight hundred miles into the trail, that after climbing over 3600 feet of elevation in seven miles, our current food supply wasn't cutting it. We were halfway up the climb when Optimist bonked. He was completely drained of energy and unable to keep walking. I was a good distance behind him on the climb and when I came to a flat spot about halfway up, I found him sitting on a large, table-top rock, just off the side of the trail. He had opened his pack and started eating anything he could find in his food bag, even if it meant he was eating the next two days' rations of food. There was no stopping him. He was ravished and not walking any further until he pumped more energy into his system. I have never seen him so exhausted. It actually scared me a little to see a bit of crazy in his eyes.

After that day, we bumped our average mileage up from about twenty-two miles a day to twenty-five, just so we could finish the section sooner in order to reach the next town, Tuolumne Meadows. It was a double-edged sword, to either burn more calories in order to get to food sooner, or to take it slower but reach town later and risk running out of food.

The section from Kennedy Meadows to Tuolumne Meadows, a lot of which runs through Yosemite National Park, ran us ragged. The elevation map of the section is testament to the tough terrain, vertically zigzagging up and down the page, just as a seismograph does when an earthquake hits. Each day we were faced with thousand foot climbs and descents, and it showed. We both lost most of our weight in that two hundred and thirty-seven mile section, going to bed each night with growling stomachs and waking each morning to a tightening of the belts. With higher elevations also came cooler temperatures, so not only were we burning extra calories on the hard climbs in the daytime, our bodies were also burning more calories to keep us warm in the evenings. I have never felt more exhausted, nor looked it, as the day we reached the other end of the tunnel at Tuolumne Meadows.

We learned our lesson the hard way. Harder climbing, higher elevations, and cooler temperatures meant we needed more quality food, with denser calories, in higher quantities. Candy bars simply were not enough, or at least we could never figure out how to pack enough of them for the energy we were extending.

Our resupply strategy changed once we reached Truckee, California, just after eleven hundred miles. We were around Lake Tahoe and had been hungry for the last four hundred miles. The days leading into Truckee were spent planning out the rest of the trip's meals, vowing to never experience another Pinchot Pass day. We took tips that we had learned thus far from other hikers who were able to carry relatively light packs, but still eat enough energy to hike a large amount of miles. Truckee also offered several large grocery stores that had lots of options, something that we hadn't experienced for weeks.

We overhauled our resupply strategy from relying solely on the towns along the way, to sending ahead boxes of food for the remaining miles of the trail. The small, expensive selection found in most of the tiny trail towns along the way had worn on us and we were ready to control what we ate the rest of the way. Thus far, the small towns had been great for a quick snack, but for an entire resupply, the options were limiting on the pallet and the prices were limiting on the wallet.

In Truckee we stocked up at both a natural foods store and a large grocery store. We packed high calorie, dense foods such as granola and gorp (good old raisins and peanuts, and chocolate chips). Then we added in food that cooked fast, such as dehydrated refried beans, angel hair pasta, rice, dehydrated mashed potatoes, and couscous. Lastly, we splurged on items that were worth their weight in flavor and overall quality of life, such as cheese and spices. I never knew how much I loved black pepper and parmesan cheese on my angel hair pasta noodles until I ate it in the middle of the woods after a hard day's hike.

We sent the food ahead to the post offices for the rest of the trail and upon arrival in each town, bought snacks and supplements as needed, depending on what our taste buds wanted. It was the change our resupply strategy needed and it greatly enhanced the quality of life on the trail going forward.

Before the trail, I never understood just how good food can be, how badly I can crave it, or just how irritable I can be when I'm truly in need of it. I never understood any of these things until I spent months on the trail facing these realizations and hearing them as my stomach screamed in protest for not being fed enough.

Many of my trail memories, my trail stories, and my trail happiness revolve around food. Eating is a fabulous addition to the story of walking. While walking was our main purpose each day, eating was the highlight of every moment spent perched on the side of the trail for a snack break, or relaxed at camp with water boiling in promise of a warm, briefly-filling meal. Towns were defined by products available for consumption and word traveled fast up and down the trail if a restaurant had a particularly positive eating experience. The days that we hiked into town were usually spent daydreaming of menus of the much-anticipated restaurants and stores.

Second to water, food was what I thought about most of the time. I constantly pictured different foods in my mind, depending on what time of day it was, how warm it was, or just what kind of mood I was in. In the hot Southern California heat, all I craved was salt, such as potato chips, pretzels, crackers…anything covered in that wonderful white sprinkling. In the cooler temperatures in Washington, my taste buds demanded chocolate and I obliged them with chocolate covered espresso beans, M&Ms and Reece's Pieces. The two foods I distinctly craved the most were Sunkist soda and Lay's wavy plain potato chips. The last time I drank a Sunkist before the trail was likely after a soccer game in eighth grade, a fresh orange can plucked out of a cooler of melting ice, bobbing among Big Reds and grape sodas.

I have no idea where the Sunkist craving came from. My only explanation, as so many other women use for strange cravings, was that it was my pregnant time.

I thought of the trail as my pregnant time, the time when I could eat whatever I wanted, in whatever quantity I wanted (as long as I was in a town of course). I have not yet been pregnant, but my take on it is that women tend to have cravings beyond any reasonable explanation, to the point where the craving will not end until it is quenched. Also during pregnancy, extra calories must inevitably be taken in. The trail miles were my reasoning for eating whatever I wanted and I still lost weight because of all the miles I walked. It really was every woman's dream.

There was an exact moment when I realized I could use the trail as an opportunity to eat whatever I wanted. It was when I was lying in my sleeping bag after two weeks on the trail. I was lying on my side and for the first time in too many years to remember, my inner thighs didn't touch. My knees were the only parts of my upper legs that touched. The rest of my inner thighs left a gaping hole where the normal fat easily found a home. My hands had lost their warming station that had been my inner thigh fat.

It was a glorious moment. I was free from calorie counting for a brief period in my life and that is one of my best memories of the PCT. Part of me wonders if only a woman could really appreciate that freedom, but I know that many men would give up some piece of their life to have that slice of life without the guilt.

That moment was when the real fun began. I made it my mission to eat as much food as I could that was off-limits in normal life, such as pizza, ice cream and chips. As long as I was still losing weight at the same time, I gave myself free reign. Up until that point, I had only heard legendary stories from Optimist, Animal and Rocketcop of being able to eat an entire pizza in one sitting and still lose weight while thru-hiking. I hoped that I would be able to experience the same feats. What person doesn't want a free pass to be able to eat whatever they want, in however many quantities they want, and still lose weight at the same time?

At the same time that I realized the trail was my chance to consume without consequence, a drastic shift occurred. My views on food changed.

Imagine the life of a thru-hiker. You have finished walking thirty miles for the day. You are tired, hungry to say the least, and you know that the same amount of hard miles awaits you tomorrow. Food has been on your mind all day, as your body never stops burning calories. You probably started today with an energy bar, you ate handfuls of granola or trail mix throughout the day, and had a bowl of pasta for lunch. You have been thinking about dinner for at least the last ten miles.

You sit down on a log and open your pack to decide what is for dinner. You know the contents of your stuff sack of food like you know your social security number or your phone number. Just like listing off those numbers, you can spout off your food bag's contents without any hesitation or thought, because you have already memorized what is available to eat and how it should be rationed over the next seven days' worth of hiking. It comes as no surprise that your choices for dinner are a variety of packaged rice dishes with different flavorings like cheddar cheese and alfredo sauce. There is only one for each day's dinner and you are so far from town that you cannot risk eating two and running out of food. You must ration. If you start snacking on the trail mix after dinner as you sit around the campfire, you will not be able to stop yourself. Only take a handful, then step away from the food bag. Again, you must ration.

This was the mental and physical battle I fought each and every day. It was maddening that I could eat whatever I wanted because of the thousands of calories I was burning each day, yet I could not eat whatever I wanted because I was on a trail, in the middle of nowhere, rationing my food for ten days at a time.

The lifestyle of losing weight from walking so many miles, coupled with rationing food because it was just too darn heavy to carry all I wanted to eat, changed me. It changed the way I looked at food, both on and off the trail. It also changed how I ate food when in the presence of seemingly endless quantities of it, such as in town or grocery stores.

It even made me a bit of crazy.

Sometimes just the anticipation of food, on the days we were reaching a town, turned me into a bumbling buffoon. I would nearly run down the trail to reach the town as fast as possible. I'd often not even talk to Optimist, much less other hikers. I knew my purpose and would not let anyone stand in my way.

The interesting thing about this shift in views on food is that it only applies to the hikers. The people already in town, who are working in the restaurants or shopping at the grocery stores, simply do not relate. Food is easily accessible for them. Sure, they get excited about the thought of chocolate chip ice cream too, but they don't run down the frozen food aisle and kiss the glass cases. They don't revel in the availability of six different types of potato chips, they don't moan at the first gulp of a freshly opened can of Sprite. They certainly don't stop in every restaurant possible throughout the course of one day. Thru-hikers freshly in town must be quite the sight.

There was even a hiker who was named after his love of food. Free Refill's name came about because of his fascination with America's offering of free refills of soft drinks in restaurants. He was German and loved Coca-Cola.

Later up the trail, we were treated to a free buffet breakfast at the Timberline Lodge, near the border of Oregon and Washington. You would not have known that the buffet was for *all* the patrons in the room and not just for our group of six hikers. Snowman alone ate his own personal plate of bacon. He cleared the contents of the buffet's bacon at least twice, not giving a second thought to taking the entire supply despite forty other people in the restaurant.

This was what we did when in the presence of food. Hunger took over logic. Behavior that in normal circumstances was downright wrong, or would at least get you shunned from quite a few social circles, somehow seemed perfectly acceptable when in the context of a thru-hike. There was a loss of a sense of civility, a sense of hygiene, and one was out of touch with any rules of normal life that applied to trail life.

Many, many times, this was the case.

One evening in Southern California, Optimist cooked one of our favorite meals, dehydrated refried beans topped with corn chips and fresh cheddar cheese. I set up the tent as he cooked the meal. After I finished and waited for dinner, I sat on a legless picnic bench that rose just an inch off the ground. As I sat there, I inspected my feet, my toes, and my healing blisters. I am the type that if I have a scab, I will pick it. Reviewing my blisters was something I loved to do in the evening during camp time.

I must have been deep in thought, because apparently, Optimist said to me as I distractedly picked at my blisters, "Stopwatch, your bowl is just to the left of you."

Not hearing this, I stood up to grab my water bottle and planted my left hand on the rim of my bowl, tipping it over and spilling half the contents on the bench, the bench from which I had just flicked away a pesky ant.

I didn't think. I hurriedly scooped the spilled contents back into the bowl, desperate to save my dinner. I didn't know if I was actually going to eat the spilled beans, but scooping them back in the bowl seemed like the right thing to do. It was what my stomach said to do. It's what Optimist's eyes said to do as he looked at me in shock because of what

I had just done, and in apprehension as he realized he might have to share his half with me.

Tears welled up in my eyes as I looked at the mess I was left with in my bowl. I no longer wanted the contents, knowing half of them were contaminated with bench germs. On the other hand, I was so hungry. It was also too early in our resupply leg to use up another meal. We had to ration until we knew for sure we'd have enough food until the next town. I knew it would be asking too much to eat half of Optimist's food because I had not noticed my bowl sitting right next to me.

I did what most other desperately hungry hikers would do. I ate the beans which seconds before had been splayed out over the picnic bench. Once the decision was made, I cleared my head of visions of tapeworms and unidentified bacteria, and enjoyed the warm, flavorful meal. I went to sleep with a full stomach and never woke up with any sickness.

With a shift in how food is viewed, and the driver's seat importance food takes in one's life, priorities in towns inevitably changed. What probably seemed important to some patrons in restaurants, such as a shower to relieve my outdoorsy scent, was simply not on my radar. Food always came first. Everything else, including bathing, could wait.

We arrived in Truckee, California on day fifty-two, just before the halfway point of the trail. Optimist's cousin picked us up from the trail at nine in the morning, after we'd hiked a mere six miles for the day. She was excited to hear our stories and to help us revel in our town time. Her first question, or statement, as she rolled down the windows was, "You guys must want a shower!"

Optimist, sitting in the passenger seat next to her, looked ready to agree, but my priorities took over and I sheepishly asked if we could stop at a bakery first before heading home. It was the first time we had ever reached a town in the early morning and I had thought about pastries and coffee since lying in the tent the evening before. I had also only had one hot shower in those first fifty-two days, so I could see why she would suggest a shower first.

Although surprised and probably slightly appalled, she obliged and stopped at one of her favorite bakeries in town.

After standing at the bakery counter undecided for some minutes, I opted for a blueberry turnover and a cheese danish for myself, along with a large hazelnut-flavored coffee. As Optimist reached for his wallet to pay, the bag of pastries was like a hot potato in my hands. I just had to do something with it. I quietly pulled the blueberry turnover about an inch out of the bag and tried to sneak in a bite before putting it in the bag for good.

I didn't think anyone was watching me. Then I looked up as I was tearing off a corner of the turnover. The guy working behind the counter looked at me in disbelief, his eyes darting between my face and my hands, and said, "There's a sink over there if you'd like to wash your hands."

It took me a second to understand what he was implying. I saw no connection with how washing my hands made eating my turnover any more possible. If anything, it detracted from it.

When I looked down at my hands, actually looking at my nails, my knuckles and my palms, I realized how much dirt had accumulated in the lines and crevices. It looked gross to see me touching food. I glanced over at the sink that looked so far away and looked back at my pastry that was so close to me. Though I was ready to decline his offer, for his sake and at his suggestion, I dutifully scrubbed away the top layer of dirt before taking my first taste of sugary blueberries and buttery pastry.

Much of the time, upon arriving in town, I could easily be mistaken for a homeless person. I was dirty, ragged, in search of food, and carrying my life on my back. Despite looking homeless, I certainly never felt that I fit the mold. I never asked anyone for money or food, though I gladly accepted free food, and I could pay for anything I wanted.

That being said, there was an evening when Optimist and I crossed the boundaries of civility and felt the shame that came with resorting to desperate measures for food.

One of our best meals on the trail was in Northern California, at a campground called Drakesbad Guest Ranch. The on-site restaurant was known for its many course meals of freshly baked breads, vegetables, and desserts. After several loaves of bread and oil as an appetizer, the main course was stuffed red peppers, along with a side of roasted vegetables, including carrots, asparagus and potatoes. For dessert they ran out of chocolate mousse before reaching us and though we were upset, we were still served deliciously satisfying raspberry sherbet.

Here comes the tipping point.

The patrons at the table next to us received two of the last servings of chocolate mousse. I covetously eyed their desserts and was appalled to see them leave their table for good, leaving behind the two servings of untouched mousse. It nearly goes without saying that they were obviously not hikers.

My eyes darted around the space, looking for any witnesses that might see me take the mousse. I saw waitresses milling around and acted before one of them approached the table to clear it for the next patrons. It pained me to see the chocolate mousse go to waste, especially because I missed out on its short supply. Without contemplating the matter further, I made like a scavenger and snagged both bowls off the table. I wasn't sure if I was really going to go through with eating them once I had grabbed them, but I at least wanted the choice.

I admitted to Optimist that I had perhaps committed a social crime, but he too was ecstatic to have a bowl of chocolate mousse sitting in front of him. We laughed the situation off, a little nervously that we had gone to such measures, and enjoyed the dessert without rethinking the decision. It simply seemed like the right thing to do, and even if it wasn't, hunger yet again trumped logic.

Optimist and I looked battle worn and exhausted by the state of Washington. I had gone from one hundred and thirty-five pounds to one hundred and ten, and Optimist from one hundred and forty-five pounds to one hundred and twenty. Maybe our thin frames, coupled with our dirty faces and legs, prompted others to give us food. Maybe there were so few of us thru-hikers going through Washington at that time, as most others never made it that far, that people were excited to see us. Whatever the reason, almost all the day hikers and weekenders that we met gave us food. Most people offered up food from their packs almost immediately after meeting us.

There was a point near Mt. Adams, early on in Washington, where we met a group of boy scouts on the last night of their trip. Their scout leader sat around our campfire with us after all the boys had gone to bed and shared pieces of his newly unwrapped block of parmesan cheese. Fresh ingredients like cheese, fruits, and vegetables were not common for us. Optimist and I were happy to be given even a sliver of the cheese. I tried to hide my excitement as I watched him carefully cut off each shaving with his small pocket knife. I was like a dog in anticipation of a feeding, already looking forward to the next piece as I ate my current one.

As the scout leader was leaving, he handed over the rest of the cheese, along with bags of trail mix, chocolate and nuts that the boy scouts thought we might like. After we thanked him with astonished gratitude, he left for his tent. Once I knew he left for good, I gave up on cutting off slivers and simply bit into the block of cheese. Optimist and I took turns in enjoying fresh parmesan by the mouthful. My cheeks ached with chewing each bite of the hard, salty, and subtly rich cheese, and it was all the more amazing of how unselfish the boy scouts had been in giving us all their extra food.

Each time that events like this occurred, I mentally relived that day on the Appalachian Trail in the Shenandoah National Park, when I had no understanding of strangers giving hikers their food. Only this time, I was on the receiving end. It was humbling to have switched places with a stranger that I had loathed so many years prior for simply being who he was, a thru-hiker. I had no idea what he was going through then, nor that I'd be going through the same thing years later, hoping others would be as generous as Optimist had been that day. The overwhelming feeling of selfishness hit me every time strangers' acts of selflessness reminded me that I had been in their position at one point, and had chosen to not share. It was embarrassing to both remember the self that I was those years back and to willingly accept food from strangers when I knew I didn't display the same act of kindness when given the chance. At that point, I could only vow to shed my selfish self and to avoid hypocrisy in accepting favors but never returning them.

Despite all the cravings and the hunger experienced along the way, despite all my complaining to Optimist that I wanted more food, I really was a consumption machine. Taking into account my daily rations of food from each resupply, along with the food I managed to fit in my stomach in each town, my caloric resume was quite impressive. Sometimes after eating, I'd look down at my belly and think, "Where does it all go?"

After finishing the trail, I was actually disappointed that I didn't eat more pizza, ice cream, or all the other foods that are off-limits on a regular basis. I felt like I got the short end of the stick in my trail eating experiences, when in reality, I was living quite lavishly. For me, if I was still losing weight after consuming as much as I did, it was my sign that

I should have been eating more. I at least learned quickly into the trail the all-important lesson that food was a wonderful thing. Having discovered my love for food, I was able to fully reap all the benefits of living out the lesson down to every last bite.

Just like water, I'm not sure many people realize the amazing availability we have to not only a large amount of food, both fresh and processed, but also to a large variety of food. I'm still overwhelmed when I walk down the aisles of most grocery stores. I'm stunned by the endless shelves of opportunities to fulfill our bodies' needs and wants with just the swipe of a credit card and a car to carry us back and forth.

I often think to myself, "Man, this would have been an awesome store to have on the trail." It's the same feeling I get when standing in awe in front of a faucet of readily available water at the twist of a knob. I'm not quite sure those around me know how good we have it.

There was an evening in the middle of Washington when Optimist and I were staying at a friend's home for the evening. I distinctly remember two inspiring moments. One was when I stood in front of the walk-in pantry, just taking in the beauty of shelves of food. I didn't even want to eat the food. It was just an amazing sight to see a closet full of food, waiting to be consumed. The second moment was when we re-discovered one of the greatest inventions of man: pizza delivery. We had a pizza delivered right to the door; we didn't have to walk to it and we didn't have to drive to it. All we had to do was pick up the phone and then wait for someone to bring it right to our door, and it was still steaming hot. Amazing.

I feel lucky to have been on both sides of the spectrum of knowing hunger, yet still being able to fulfill it. While I dealt with constant hunger, I always knew a town was within reach. I always knew that patience was my best friend and that the time of hunger from a thru-hike would end. I didn't like it, but I knew it was self-imposed. I knew it had an ending. I knew endless days of trips to the grocery store, and pantries and refrigerators full of food, awaited me at the end of the trail. I knew my life would return to normal after the trail and I could have as many sodas and bags of chips as I wanted. Only it wouldn't be as much fun. I'd actually have to worry about calories once again.

Because of the trail, my views on food have morphed even more since finishing. The appreciation and love for food is still there, but not the craze that came with the anticipation of eating or obtaining it. While it would have been devastating on the trail, I rarely find myself getting upset if a certain item is unavailable at the grocery store. When

I see a blank space where my favorite brand of fudge brownie ice cream once lived, I shrug my shoulders and either go without or choose one of other endless options.

An item being unavailable was the story of my life on the trail. Nothing was ever available when I wanted it. I couldn't order take out, there was no delivery, and there definitely weren't drive-thru windows. My only choices for food were what I was willing to carry, and while it was maddening at moments, it taught me patience and planning. It also taught me to get my fill while I could in town, because the cravings were guaranteed to catch right back up with me once I stepped on the trail.

In my life today, there is always the knowledge that I will not go hungry. I can both afford to buy food and I live in a country with readily available options in each town, on each corner, and in each building. Try and spend a day of life *not* seeing an opportunity to eat or purchase food. In circumstances other than walking in the middle of the woods, I doubt it can be done.

Perhaps you didn't need a reminder of just how good food is. I certainly did, as it was a blunt slap in the face to start hiking and be cursed with endless stomach growls and cravings. Though I counted calories before the trail, true rationing had never been part of my lifestyle before thru-hiking and I certainly never had to wait days until reaching another town for food. In my everyday life, I think back to those moments on the trail when I would have given anything to eat the meal sitting in front of me at this very moment, and I'm forever grateful for the plate of food that was so easily obtained and which is so satisfyingly filling. I'm usually even more thankful that I didn't have to walk hundreds of miles to get it.

Julie Urbanski

4 LESS IS MORE

Especially when you are carrying it on your back for over 2600 miles.

Imagine you are told to pack for a trip. Yes, that sounds simple enough. The first questions that might go through your mind are, "Where am I going and how long is the trip?"

Well, you are going through the desert, through snow, through forests, and lastly, through rainy, muddy terrain. The trip in total is over 2600 miles. It will last as long as you want it to, but usually requires around four to five months if you want to complete it.

It sounds tough to plan, but you've packed suitcases for trips before, so you dive right in.

As you start sifting through your closet, making piles on the bed for shirts, pants, socks, underwear, jackets, shoes, toiletries... you think to yourself, "This isn't so bad. I'll just prepare for every scenario so I'm ready for whatever is thrown at me."

Then, as you look through the garage for that old reliable suitcase on wheels, you are told that all these clothes must fit into a knapsack half the size your pillow case.

In addition, you can forget the wheels, because everything you bring will be carried in a backpack. Be sure to leave plenty of room for food and water, because you'll be carrying those items too, for all 2600 miles.

Suddenly, you are back to square one. You are not sure where to begin. Each item of clothing has to be carefully considered and the weeding out process becomes much harder. It seems downright impossible to have a small sack of clothing to last for four months, let alone carry it and all of life's other necessities on your back for that long too.

This is the life of a thru-hiker. Weight in the pack is a hiker's worst enemy, and every single item must be considered for both the space it takes up in the pack, and the weight it adds. Keeping the pack weight to a bare minimum is one of the greatest challenges posed to thru-hikers. I know of very few, if any, who have fought the battle of pack weight and come out unscathed, because every pound in the pack is one too many.

There is much thought that goes into choosing not only clothing, but also every single pound, and even ounce, that enters the pack. It is more than just pure desire and enjoyment that deem what enters a pack. This is even truer when it comes to food. I would have loved to pick up a twelve-pack of soda at every point possible, but it was hardly feasible to carry. It is utility and weight that matter, and many items do not make the cut.

It is the constant fear of adding too much weight to the pack that makes most hikers' decisions of what to carry. This predicament, the desire to carry not only needs, but wants, without greatly increasing the pack weight, follows a hiker all the way up the trail. It is an obstacle that perhaps is never conquered, and that every hiker is constantly battling.

Before I even took one step on the PCT, one piece of advice I received ten times over from other hikers was to have the lowest possible pack weight. I definitely listened to them, but I can't say I actually practiced it very well. How could I have known what would be the best pack weight for me before even starting? Hoisting the pack up and walking around the apartment is hardly preparation for knowing how much weight is too much for a long-distance hike. It was something Optimist and I simply had to learn through trial and error.

Pack weight is just that, the weight of the pack with everything stuffed in it. People think of pack weight in terms of two different weights, one being the base weight of the items that do not change and that are completely essential (that being a relative term as well), and the other being the total weight of the pack. The essentials for me included the pack itself, a tent, a sleeping bag, and a stove...the absolute necessities in my eyes. Then there is the total pack weight that includes food, water, and other specialty items that are always changing in weight or aren't always in the pack. These items can cause the pack weight to fluctuate greatly. For example, you are going to have more food when leaving a town rather than entering one. A pack is inevitably heavier upon walking out of town, weighed down with food to last another stretch of days until the next town is reached.

As the trail continues, a hiker's definition of "essential" undergoes an unavoidable transformation. Items that seemed important when packing for a long-distance hike, such as a pocket knife for protection, a book to read in camp, or a second jacket for warmth, suddenly seem like dead weight when faced with interminable switchbacks up and down mountains passes.

No matter what terms are used to define pack weight, it's ideal to have the lowest possible number. That being said, it's also an incredibly hard ideal to live out. A low pack weight for one hiker might be twenty-five pounds. It might be forty for another. It's up to what the hiker is willing to carry and how much they want to enjoy the experience of a lighter load over thousands of miles.

There is no magic number, but there is magic in a low one.

The first day on the trail would have been hard enough had I just strapped a water bottle to my waist and nothing more. I was not in hiking shape, nor was I ready for the hot, dry climate of Southern California. It was that much harder with a heavy pack that neared thirty-five pounds and legs that weren't accustomed to walking for several hours. Throw in a few uphill climbs and I was downright miserable, cursing every pound on my back.

Thankfully, I didn't pack as badly as Animal. While I was carrying more weight than was good for me, he was carrying so much that it hurt his chances of even making it past the first day.

Despite the fact that Animal had hiked the AT, he seemed to forget everything he knew about packing. We were not with Animal the day before the trail began, or maybe we could have offered some useful, much-needed advice before we actually started walking with him. The day before we walked our first miles, he went to the local outdoors store and picked up a pair of leather, no-room-for-breathing, weighing-ten-pounds-each hiking boots. They were similar to the ones he hiked in on the AT. Those boots served him very well on the AT.

Unfortunately for Animal, we set out to hike the PCT. The first seven hundred miles of the PCT is desert conditions. It's very dusty, dry, and very hot. Ventilation is key to keeping feet happy. Heavy, leather boots typically aren't mixed with the southern portion of the PCT. That was one strike against Animal.

Before driving out to the start of the trail, Optimist, Rocketcop and I met Animal at his friend's apartment in San Diego. All three of us arrived with our trail clothes donned, shoe laces tightened, and packs ready to go.

As we sat and waited for our ride to the trail, we watched in awe as Animal gathered up the contents of his pack, most of which were sprawled out across the living room floor. I made sure my pack stayed clear of the tornado of stuff sacks and plastic bags.

After we saw Animal's newly purchased boots, the empty box being nearly the size of Rocketcop's pack, we took our seats on the floor. We all wanted front row seats to the Animal show, so we formed a circle with Animal in the middle as he sifted through his possessions. As he stuffed more items into his pack, the pack seemed to grow even larger, sprawling new pockets, crevices, and zippers.

Pockets, crevices and zippers are not good for a hiker. It is like the newlywed couple that moves from a one bedroom apartment to a four-bedroom, three-bath home. Do they really need all that space just for them? They are likely to spend money filling it up with stuff that they may never use. A large, empty pack is just as dangerous to a thru-hiker. It's just begging to be filled with useless weight.

In order to cook, Animal brought a homemade stove made out of a soda can and a tuna can. It was a surprising choice for a stove, considering the minimal weight that it added to his pack. He was very proud of his homemade stove. Perhaps as a counter to the lightness of his stove, Animal packed an entire can of fuel. This equated to about four pounds of fuel. He may have never used even half that amount over the entire length of the trail. He was ready to pack two of them, thinking we might need some. We were able to convince him that we all had in fact thought to pack an adequate amount of fuel, so he only packed one.

Animal also packed seven days' worth of food, never bothering to check the data book to see that the first store would most likely be reached within three days. He was carrying four extra days' worth of food. His logic was that seven days would surely get him to some sort of town in which to resupply.

This is great reasoning if your stuff is being carried by a car, and you have the luxury of over-packing. Luxury does not mix with long-distance backpacking. Four days of extra food weight barely affects a car's gas mileage, but is downright self-punishing in hiking. There is not a reward to those that show up in town with four extra days of food. No one will congratulate you on such a feat.

That was most of the packing that we watched with Animal. The boots were a lost cause. He would not have time to get new shoes for the desert. We tried to get him to cut down on food, but he was excited at the prospect of carrying so many candy bars, nuts and trail mix. At least we saved him the weight of an extra can of fuel. Thankfully he shed that weight, as we had no idea what else he'd shoved deeply into his pack before our arrival, never guessing what he had next.

Maybe we should have guessed, or at least inspected his pack further once we'd seen the two cans of fuel. Though he would have not been convinced, we could have at least made the case for leaving behind the next item, a fifth of Jim Beam whiskey, in a glass bottle.

We were about five miles into the trail before he pulled it out of his pack, a wide grin across his face. All of our expressions could have only shown shock. That is a picture in my mind that I will never forget, of Animal reaching deep into his pack's main compartment and pulling out his prized bottle of whiskey with excitement in his eyes and anticipation of the evening's camp.

There was even a bit of crazy in those eyes. He already had his shirt off, his fleshy chest and arms showing hints of a burn from being so bluntly uncovered to the cruel sun. Animal wore the only pair of sunglasses he could find at the last minute, a pair of women's sunglasses with round, large, dark lenses and leopard print on the side. They were pushed to the top of his head, splaying his hair out so that it pointed in every direction.

It was tried and true Animal: wild, unleashed, and unplanned, yet still so able to focus on the task at hand. He is a friend that Optimist and I truly love.

I can only laugh at this point. It's a moment that I think of randomly throughout my days. I smile to myself as I remember not only Animal's entire look, but also our stunned reaction as he revealed one of his pack's discretionary items. My first thought when I saw the whiskey was, "What else does he have in that pack?"

It's hard to believe, but he certainly had more.

It seemed that with each ensuing step, we learned just how poorly Animal had packed.

Rocketcop, Optimist and I reached camp around eight o'clock that first day, when the sun was setting and we were losing daylight quickly.

Animal was behind us. We didn't know by how much, or if he would even make it to camp. All we could think about was water, dinner and sleep. Optimist made dinner as the daylight faded and we set up camp. When he turned on his headlamp, it was already dead. His headlamp must have been on in his pack all day, running the batteries dead before he'd even had the chance to use it in the dark.

Luckily my headlamp still worked, so Optimist used mine as I felt around in the enclosing darkness to put up our tent.

Animal didn't show up for another hour, waking us as his headlamp flitted erratically over the ground and our tents. Optimist was quick to pop up and zip open the tent's door, emerging excitedly as Animal settled into camp. I stayed in the tent, also glad that he had made it, but too tired to move any more than necessary.

Optimist immediately helped Animal set up his tent and cook his dinner, but he couldn't see much without his headlamp. He hadn't come back into our tent to get mine, and Animal noticed that Optimist was trying to help him blindly.

"Optimist, where's your headlamp?"

"It must have been on in my pack all day. The batteries are completely dead," Optimist explained.

"Oh, well here, I have two headlamps. Take this one!"

As he eagerly dug into his pack, which was now seeming like Mary Poppins' bottomless purse, all three of us in unison, Rocketcop, Optimist and I, were abruptly woken out of our half-stupor as we exclaimed, "YOU HAVE TWO HEADLAMPS!?!"

What Animal was doing with two headlamps as a single thru-hiker, I will never know. The weight of one headlamp is enough. The weight of a second is completely unjustified, even if it was handy that one could be lent to Optimist. Again, I can only quietly chuckle at this point, my head shaking in disbelief at how poorly Animal had packed despite having already hiked a long-distance trail.

I can only guess how heavy Animal's pack was that first day. I would say it was somewhere between sixty and seventy pounds. The strange thing was, as he sat down for dinner that first night, he realized he didn't bring a cooking pot. I'm not sure where the logic was in bringing an entire can of fuel, a bottle of whiskey, two headlamps, and who knows what other useless stuff, yet no vessel in which to cook food. Lucky for Animal, we *over*-packed in that department. We had two cooking pots, the smaller of which we quickly parted with in order to lessen our load and make his eating possible.

Though Animal was a prime example of how not to pack, he was not the exception. Many hikers struggle under the weight of an overstuffed pack. Optimist and I counted ourselves among that group for quite some time.

Within the first ten days of the trail, Optimist and I were also known as Team Sherpa. We were bestowed this name by Tatu Jo, a huge proponent of ultralight backpacking, with the evidence to back it up. He's broken the speed record for hiking the trail in the fewest number of days on more than one occasion, and I'm sure a light pack certainly helped his odds of being able to hike an average of over forty miles a day.

Our packs were easily double the size of Tatu's, and felt that way too. While his weighed around fifteen to twenty-five pounds, ours were thirty to fifty. Almost every time we ran across him along the trail, he managed to get in a comment about our huge packs.

Not only was my pack weight heavy, but the pack itself, without anything in it, already weighed at least four pounds, which is a few pounds too many. I refused to purchase a new pack before hiking the PCT, as I had a perfectly good one (or so I thought) that I'd bought for a trip prior to even considering a long-distance hike. My pack looked as good as any to hike with. I filled it up, threw it over my shoulders, tightened the hip belts, and started walking, quickly realizing the importance of base weight. I could never change the weight of my pack, so I had to look towards my pack contents when deciding where to cut weight.

Optimist and I actually thought we would have the energy and the desire to read at camp, so he brought a hardback copy of Marcel Proust's *Swann's Way*. I brought a paperback copy of Leo Tolstoy's work, *Anna Karenina*. Those books quickly found their way home on day three when we reached the Mt. Laguna Post Office. They were never missed.

That was five pounds sent home right there.

By the time we made it to day ten, when we met Optimist's brother in town, I had other items that I knew I wanted to get rid of that were weighing me down. It was my first chance to unload unnecessary pack weight and I had plenty of time to think about it. Optimist and I evaluated the contents of our packs often, considering what could be sent home and what was absolutely necessary. It was one of my common distractions while I was walking all day, mentally calculating how much weight I could get rid of at the next post office. When all I had to do was walk all day and all I could think about was how hard it was, I inevitably thought of ways to make it easier without downright quitting.

I would question myself, "Do I really need this _____ (insert most items here)?" If I answered no, then I rid myself of that item the next chance I got, which was the next garbage can, hiker-box, or self-addressed box at the post office. Once the realization hit that an item was not necessary, it was hard to justify keeping it much longer in the pack.

If I found myself answering yes to actually needing the item, I asked, "Is there a better way to fulfill my need for this item without so much weight?" I would most likely answer yes to this as well, as many items can serve multiple purposes. My blue bandana never failed as a towel, sun protection on my neck, a pot holder, or a dish towel.

For some reason I thought I would want clean underwear on the hike, so I packed three pair of "hiking" underwear that were the wicking, non-cotton material. I found by day three that no underwear at all was the best policy. Not only was it cooler to go commando in the hot section of Southern California, for the occasional breeze created a nice air current, it was also easier to pee. I only had one layer to drop down and pull up in a much more fluid motion. Underwear always found a way to get caught on my knees or thighs, increasing the chances of me flashing another hiker as I struggled to pull up two layers at once.

Along with two pair of underwear, as I kept one for my "town" underwear in order to feel a little more civilized when we were among people, I unloaded one of two sports bras, a long sleeve shirt, two pair of super thick socks, a water pump, and a towel. Optimist's brother took all of our unnecessary items back to his home in Los Angeles.

I'm sure there were many more things in my pack that I could have unloaded, but just those items alone made a big difference in my hiking. It's amazing how much more enjoyable the experience is and how much easier an uphill is, when shoulders and hips aren't groaning under the weight of items that are unnecessary.

Although we were quick to drop pack weight in the beginning, Optimist and I still struggled under the weight of our packs for much of the first half of the trail.

After much cajoling and reasoning from other hikers in Old Station, California, around mile 1377, Optimist and I were convinced to seriously evaluate our pack weight. When actually faced with parting with items, it was harder than it should have been. I grew very attached to my pack contents, justifying their weight by how much use I got out of them. It's amazing how hard it is to part with just stuff, whether it's necessary or not.

We shed items that I hadn't even considered as dead weight, such as the top-loader on my pack, the case that held my pack cover, extra stuff sacks, an extra first aid kit, and several other random items that somehow amounted to thirteen pounds between Optimist and me.

We were shocked to find that we were carrying around that much dead weight between the two of us. After that point, we vowed to each other to only carry what was absolutely necessary (in our eyes, that's the catch) and to shun the attachment to luxury items.

Compared to others like Tatu Jo, we were still Team Sherpa, but compared to our old selves in the first few weeks, we were downright minimalists. Since we were only around Tatu Jo in Southern California, when our packs were at their heaviest, we never got the chance to redeem ourselves in showing him just how much our pack weight had changed over the course of the trail. We renamed ourselves to Team Sherpa Light by the time we reached Oregon, when we had matured enough in our packing abilities to dare put the word light in our team title.

Old Station, California ended up being a turning point not only in our pack weight, but also in my general enjoyment of the trail. The trail is hard enough to walk without anything in excess of clothing, so adding a thirty pound pack can make it nearly unbearable. What I didn't realize in the beginning of the trail was that less is more not only because a lighter pack makes for an easier hike, but also because a lighter pack makes for a more enjoyable experience.

I didn't realize that because hiking with a heavy pack was so hard on me, because my gear was literally weighing me down physically and mentally, I wasn't enjoying the experience as a whole. The experience of living as a long-distance hiker. The experience of having my days to myself, of living outside, and of feeling free of any obligations besides those that I self-imposed.

There is something magical and uplifting about staring off into the distance at the top of a mountain pass or across a pristine lake. In the beginning, my head hung so low under my pack weight that I was busy staring at the ground instead of looking out and taking in my surroundings. My suffering through the daily miles under a heavy pack spread its ugly, pessimistic tentacles to the other parts of the trail: the camp time and town time with Optimist and other hikers, the alone time with myself that I could have used to think rather than whine about the difficulty of the hike, and the simple time to look out across the mountains and inhale the experience swirling around me. I was missing out on the actual trail experience because of stuff.

Life changed after my pack weight changed. I understood the pull of a long distance hike. I understood why people did these sorts of things so willingly and why they talked of them so enthusiastically. I began to focus on myself, on my relationship with Optimist, on my relationship with the trail, and the miles really did get easier both physically and mentally. Once I cut the cord that was binding me to my things, it was easy to forget about them and focus on the experiences that were happening in the present. I was able to salvage the second half of the trail and actually became a slight optimist. I'm embarrassed it took me almost half the trail to enjoy it, but at least I realized it early enough that I could enjoy that much of it.

Still, however avoidable it may seem to others, everyone has their luxury items. The items that make no logical sense in why they have taken up permanent residency in a pack. Once they've taken up that space in both the pack and the hiker's heart, it is hard to convince a hiker of its useless, dead weight.

My luxury item was my potty trowel. Luckily it weighed in at just a few ounces.

My potty trowel was a bright orange shovel which I used to dig my mini toilets each time I had to unload my bowels. It only cost me $1.75 and added very little pack weight. To most other hikers, the trowel was downright silly to carry around, as many deemed it useless.

I grew to love that potty trowel. It even had measurements on it in increments of inches so I could be sure I was digging the proper, forest-friendly six-inch deep hole. I often did this effortlessly. Optimist scoffed at the potty trowel just as other hikers did, happy to use a random stick off the side of the trail for his digging instrument. Sticks really gave him trouble when the ground was dry and not conducive to digging holes, often snapping under too much pressure. While he would try to hurriedly dig a hole with bowels that had a mind of their own, I would calmly dig my six-inch deep hole, smiling happily at the trowel's bright orange contrast to the brown ground and at Optimist's struggle in denying himself of the joy of a potty trowel.

Somehow poop makes its way into many conversations among hikers, and is quite a regular occurrence with all the meals going in and the miles churning out. Making the experience all the more enjoyable through a simple, lightweight tool was absolutely worth the extra weight.

I'm sure I carried many other items that were luxury to most, and vice versa, but there were very few luxury items left by the time we were in Washington. Because those items went through countless rounds of pack weight inspections, I had a small affection for them. I loved them all the more because they had proven themselves time and again of being worthy enough to add weight to my pack, and because I had carried them so far.

I don't think I would have loved any of my pack contents at all had I been able to throw them all in a trunk and simply have my gear waiting for me at camp. Because I had to go through so much pain walking up, down and through countless mountain passes with my pack weighing on my hips and shoulders, I loved every single piece of gear in it. If I didn't love something, it would be gone at the next town, never to be missed again.

The day that I knew we had succeeded in the principle of Less is More was the day we were hiking past Timberline Lodge in Northern Oregon. There were quite a few weekenders and day hikers out on the trail, as it was a Saturday. We had just left the lodge, destined to waddle due to bellies full of pancakes, pastries and pizza. We came across a group of four older hikers going the opposite way on the trail, and they eyed us up and down as we approached them. Their eyes did not seem to approve of our filthy, worn gear and thin clothing. We looked and smelled homeless at that point, the dirt and grime having set up a permanent home on our belongings and bodies.

We had already passed the four hikers, but one of the men's curiosities got the better of him, and he turned to question us.

"How long you two been out here?"

It was a question we were always ready and willing to answer. I stopped, spun around to face him, and spoke first.

"Well, today makes eighty-eight days."

I waited for their reaction rather than give them too much information.

"What! Where'd you come from?" His voice raised an octave as all four of them now turned to question us with their forward-leaning postures.

"Mexico."

I couldn't help but smile as I said it. Optimist was grinning too, knowing this answer was perhaps more of a shock than the first.

"What? Are you two hiking the whole thing?"

Surprisingly, they at least knew a little about the trail we were walking on, as they knew there was a "whole thing" involved.

"Yep," we answered calmly.

"Well, you two don't look like thru-hikers. Your packs are too small!"

I was at first offended with his comment that we didn't look like thru-hikers. Not only did I feel like a thru-hiker then, I called myself one. I felt like a machine that was able to handle any amount of miles that were ahead of me. My anger immediately subsided when I fully processed his second comment. That's when I knew that we had learned our lesson in pack weight, that we finally achieved the goal of smaller packs.

All we could do was smile in response to his comment on our packs, for he had no idea how difficult it had been, or how long it had taken us, to prove that we had learned our lesson.

Just after finishing the trail, Optimist and I moved cross-country together from Annapolis, Maryland to Vancouver, Washington. We fit everything we needed in our one car, a Honda Element. It was so full that the driver had to wear the bike helmet in order to find a place for it. Though it wasn't exactly a comfortable ride, and it wasn't easy moving into a new apartment without a thing to furnish it, it was worth every moment of whittling down our things so that our lives could fit in one carload. It was incredibly freeing to travel so easily with our lives wrapped in one small package.

Whittling down our possessions made us look at what we had, made us decide what we actually needed, forced us to fully use the things we held on to, and lastly, made us appreciate what we actually kept. The same rounds of possession inspections that we went through on the trail allowed us to do the same in our lives, thus eliminating unnecessary life weight.

We recently moved from one apartment to another within Vancouver, and it took six carloads to move all our things. Amazingly, we had accumulated that much stuff in just a year of living in a one bedroom apartment.

When we stopped to think about it, we were embarrassed. We thought of ourselves as minimalists upon finishing the trail. It certainly didn't show in the way we lived afterwards.

Suddenly, we had become weighed down by our things. We could not just pick up and leave because we had so much *stuff* to deal with. Stuff that we'd grown attached to, stuff that we found it harder to part with, and stuff that we created a need for.

There is an overwhelming pull of attachment that comes with stuff.

It took me half the trail to realize I was jeopardizing my enjoyment of the trail because of my inability to part with things. It took us moving to a new apartment to realize that we had weighed ourselves down with possessions without even knowing it. Acquiring things was done nearly involuntarily. It wasn't noticed until it was time to clean out the cabinets, the closets and all the other hidden storage spaces.

Think back to Animal's pack being likened to a newlywed couple buying an over-sized home.

Maybe they want that big of a home. Maybe they want to and can afford to purchase items to fill it up. There is certainly nothing wrong with that scenario. However, in looking at the things that the couple chooses to fill the home with, a few more contingent items inevitably attach themselves to those things, thus creating an even bigger burden.

Say the couple buys all new furniture for the entire home, including the living room, dining room, bedrooms...the list goes on. They must have a way to pay for it, whether it is cash or credit. They most likely have to work more hours or a longer tenure in order to make that cash or pay off that credit. A home that big, with that much stuff, undoubtedly needs to be insured. Add that to the pile of add-ons and expenses that come with things. Take into account the attachment that most people find with items, and you'll find that they are fearful that someone might come along and steal those things or that friends might come over and accidentally damage them. Lastly, say they get the inclination to hike a trail. Suddenly they either have to find a way to store their things while they are gone, or find someone to look after them. And that's implying that they can even afford to stop working when bills are still steadily coming in to pay for all those things.

After all these considerations, at the end of the day, all we are talking about is *stuff*. Inanimate objects that cannot love us back. One is left to question, with all the extra efforts that go into having things, is it really worth it? Do these things really add that much more enjoyment to life that it's worth working this hard for them? These are questions I asked myself often on the trail, and ones that I ask perhaps even more often in my daily life.

Is having stuff really worth it? It's not as easy to answer, "No" as you would think. Many people, if really pressed, would probably answer, "Yes." There is nothing wrong with answering yes. But, the freedom, both mental and physical, that comes with answering no, is downright empowering. *Having* things is not as dangerous as *letting* those things rule life-decisions because the attachment to them is so strong. To not be bound by things and to cut the cord from the pull of possessions, are uplifting experiences. It allows one to focus time and energy on objects that can grow, can change, and can love you back: yourself and those around you.

Just like many other people, there are a few items that Optimist and I would hate to part with, like our paintings, our books and our photos. These are items that are all the more loved and bring that much more enjoyment to our lives because they have made it through countless rounds of possession inspections and cross-country moves.

Yet, if everything was to burn down tomorrow, and Optimist and I still had both of our lives, we could still move on. We would have to; that is what inevitably happens. We would certainly grieve the loss of our things, but since we already learned that acquiring things is a nearly involuntary act, we would have no trouble in finding more. We cannot replace each other.

Optimist and I know the freedom that comes with having very little stuff that is absolutely necessary. We know the enjoyment of the overall experience that comes with a lightened load. We are able to make the most of our lives and our relationships with ourselves, each other and our friends and family because actual things have no real place in our heart. Things are certainly fun to have, but when they get to the point of preventing life from happening to the fullest, it's time to remember that less is more.

5 SHARE WITH OTHERS

How often do you stop a stranger to find out what's on their day's agenda, let alone simply look them in the eye and say, "Hello"? Try waving to complete strangers on the sidewalk or in the car, driving down the street.

What kind of reaction do you get? You are likely to get no response at all, or that look we all know that says we're toeing the line of socially acceptable behavior.

Opening up so quickly to strangers just doesn't happen in everyday life. Nor is it widely welcomed. On the trail, it's commonplace and downright awkward when someone *doesn't* say hello or acknowledge your presence with at least a nod or a wave. It's also difficult to ignore someone when they pass within inches of you on a single-track trail, coming so close that you can smell the peanut butter on their breath.

The trail wasn't exactly a busy sidewalk where we walked with a crowd going our way or passed people going the other way. There were times when we saw a lot of people in one day, totaling about twenty, but those days were a rarity. On normal days, we saw a few people at the most. In sections of Washington, Optimist and I could go the whole day and only see each other. When we actually did cross other people's paths, we instinctively said hello and looked them in the eye. More often than not, we would stop to chat for a moment to find out where they'd come from and where they were headed.

One of the greatest luxuries on the trail is that of time. There is time to walk, to think, to eat, and to sleep. With other people comes time to share meals, stories, campfires, and of course, miles. Because there is plenty of time for all these activities, the feeling of being in a hurry simply doesn't exist.

If we were to say hello to another hiker along the trail in passing, and we heard the response, "Sorry, I can't talk right now. I'm too busy," we have would said, "With what?" When all you need to do each day, at the bare minimum, is walk, eat and sleep, it leaves the day-planner wide open for plenty of "meetings" with other hikers.

The time-crunched excuses that we use so often in daily life, such as meetings to attend, deadlines to meet, emails to write, presentations to create…simply do not exist on the trail. The only deadlines a thru-hiker worries about are the operating hours of restaurants, grocery stores and post offices, and the approaching winter season near the end of the hike.

This might sound too laid back to you, too lax. You're probably thinking, "That sounds boring. What did you do all day?" In fact, it was just the opposite, only the focus of time shifted to different priorities. While walking, eating and sleeping were the to-dos written in stone, plenty of time was left for Optimist and I to focus on our relationships with ourselves and those around us. We took advantage of the abundance of time for those few short months.

Being on the trail does something to people. It somehow binds everyone together, whether they're out there for months or just a few days. There is something about walking in the woods with your life on your back that disconnects you from the plugged-in world and connects you to the people you meet along the way.

Because of the abundance of time on one's hands, and because of the vast amount of experiences that one goes through along the trail, it's inevitable to share stories of those new experiences. There is so much to share that one might burst if not given an outlet for all the newness. Sharing cannot be helped or even avoided.

Even if there is no one physically there to tell stories to, there are places to write them down. These places are known as trail journals. Notebooks and registers are located up and down the trail for hikers to sign into. They are maintained by the greater trail community that live near the trail, or that dedicate themselves to being a part of the trail.

Some hikers note merely their name and the date when they crossed the trail journal's path. Others tell stories, write quotes, or quick blurbs about their last few days, such as, "First day without rain in three days.

Never knew how much I loved the sun." I believe I often wrote an ode to ice cream.

Trail journals are a fun way for people going north and south on the trail to read about other's experiences, to see who is around them, and to be assured that they in fact are not alone on a sometimes seemingly lonely trail. To know that others are out there, walking the same miles, sweating in the same hot sun, dealing with the same cravings for food and drink, creates a kinship.

Even if you never see their faces or hear their voices, the knowledge that you are not alone is enough to continue. Trail journals are just one piece of the puzzle that helps create that strong bond among the long-distance hiking community.

The trail would have been a completely different experience had I hiked it alone. I may have never set foot on the trail had Optimist not persuaded me (ok, convinced me after several years) to attempt the thru-hike. We shared everything with others, such as stories, views, food, campfires, campsites, photos…you name it, and someone else was part of it beside me. The trail may have been downright boring for me had I not had Optimist with me to share the views atop a mountain pass or to share in the anticipation and relish of a hot cheese pizza in town. Though the adventure would not have been worse without other people around me, my experience was greatly enhanced because I shared it with others such as Optimist and other thru-hikers, day hikers, weekenders, townspeople, and at-home family and friends.

In hiking the trail, I realized that I didn't need most of the pieces of my existing world in order to survive. While I may not have needed other people to survive, I *wanted* them around me. Not constantly, like a thirty-story apartment building in the middle of New York City, cabs honking into the wee hours. Instead, I appreciated the joy that came in sharing the experience with others in some small way, such as a meal, or an evening's campfire. Those are the times I remember most vividly. I reminisce about them the most, the times when I was looking across the campfire and seeing other trail-worn faces smiling back into mine.

The success rate of hikers completing the entire walk from Mexico to Canada is daunting. At around sixty percent, it is an eerie feeling to be part of a group at the beginning of the trail. When looking around at the faces in that group, one knows the odds are against many of the group members in making it to the end. That includes oneself. No one wants to be the first to get off the trail, whether by choice or situation.

Since I started with a group of four people, including myself, Optimist, Rocketcop and Animal, I knew we either had to defy the odds for all of us to finish, or else someone was going home before the Canadian border. I just didn't want it to be me.

Our group lasted all of one day and one night together. We found out pretty quickly how accurate those odds were.

Starting on day two, we were down to three.

As you already know, the first day was rough for Animal. An overladen pack full of seven days' worth of food, a fifth of whiskey in a glass bottle, a four pound can of stove fuel, two headlamps, and who knows what other excessive weight, were all part of the cause. In addition, the blisters on his feet were visual proof of the fault in buying heavy, leather boots the day before a trail that began in the desert.

Even with all that against him, we weren't too worried. He'd thruhiked the Appalachian Trail with relative ease and without much preparation. He was just a bit more out of shape and a tad less prepared than ideal at the beginning of a long-distance hike. Animal had overcome far more hardships in life than blisters and a heavy pack, so we assumed the trail could only get easier for him.

On the morning of the second day, Animal told us to go ahead without him. He wanted to visit a camp store down the road from the campground where we stayed, hoping to shed pack weight, nurse his blisters, and catch us later that day. We had no doubt that we would see him that evening.

He never showed.

For the next few days, we left notes along the trail, telling Animal where we'd be camping for the night. We hoped he was right behind us and simply taking his time in catching up. It became a common joke among the three of us that one night, somewhere in Northern California, Animal would finally catch up with us as we sat down to dinner, throwing his pack to the ground in exhaustion, looking at us with hungry eyes and filthy clothes, growling out, "There you are, you sons o' bitches!"

It became a joke only because we wished it would happen. Each night our hope would renew itself as we glanced back towards the trail, willing Animal to catch up. He was a good friend that we'd hoped to spend most of the trail with, and it was sad when he never appeared. We were certainly worried, but our cell phones didn't work, and since we didn't know if he was even on the trail, it would have been useless to walk backwards to find out. Animal was on his own. We just hoped that he was ok with that predicament.

It wasn't until day nine that our cell phones had reception. We had a voicemail from Animal. He never got back on the trail that second day. He was picked up by his cousin who had dropped us off just the day before, and was nursing his blisters back in San Diego before he'd try getting on the trail again.

So it was that we only had one day and one night on the trail with Animal. Though it was only a day, it was still a day full of experiences we shared, from finding our way to the start of the trail, to sweating in the high noon heat of the desert, to arriving to a bone-dry Hauser Creek at mile sixteen, to realizing that melted chocolate bars were not good food to carry in the heat, to walking twenty miles on our first day, to finally falling asleep in never-before-experienced exhaustion. There are plenty of stories to tell just from that one day.

Animal ended up carving his own trail experience, getting back on the trail and hiking about five hundred miles before ending his thru-hike attempt for good. He made just as many friends and memories as we did, only the trip in total fell a little short on the mileage. While it wasn't a complete thru-hike, it was Animal's experience all of his own.

Perhaps it was better that I learned quickly that things constantly change, people get on and off the trail, and the only thing to count on until the end is that it's going to be a long, hard journey from Mexico to Canada. Losing Animal so quickly made us grateful for the presence of others around us, and it opened my eyes to the excitement in meeting new people along the way. More often than not, the best place to soak in time with others was at camp time.

One part of my day that I especially looked forward to was camp time. For me, camp time meant sitting down, taking my shoes off my mile-worn feet, eating a much-awaited dinner, and spending time with others. We spent camp time with thru-hikers, day hikers, weekenders, family members, and just ourselves. We shared stories, talked trail strategies, sorted out the world's problems, discussed other life adventures, and suggested good books to read. Nothing was off limits when it came to camp talk.

There is a lot to learn about others, and countless topics to touch on, when there is no such thing as TV or internet to infringe on that precious time. The minutes tick by slowly when there are no distractions to waste them. Quality of relationships begins to matter so much more than any quantity, though time does allow for both along the trail. Had most of us not been so exhausted from the miles we were covering, we could have talked all night rather than falling asleep in each evening's oncoming darkness.

The amazing thing about sharing camp time with others was that the actual camp location didn't matter. Despite popular assumptions, there were very few campgrounds along the way. Whatever place looked like a good stopping point, we called it home for the evening. As long as we had water, there was a flat patch of ground, and it wasn't in a wind-blown location, we were ready to call it a night. We could have cared less whether we had a scenic spot by the lake or a site nestled among the trees. When you're only calling it home from about 7:30 p.m. to 5:30 a.m., it's just not necessary to waste time in staking out the best spot for the night. I could have passed out just about anywhere, and usually did.

We ran the gamut of campsites, from plush spots with piped water to sites ridden with cow poop. Despite the wide range of spots, we enjoyed the company we were with just the same.

A memorable campsite was that spent with Optimist's younger brother, Jeff. It was day eleven when we met Jeff in Southern California. Having hiked half of the AT in 2004, he wanted to see how the hiking on the PCT compared to that on the East Coast. He planned on hiking with us one day, and then turning around the next to get back to his car.

On the day we hiked out of town, after a difficult sixteen miles full of oppressive heat and challenging climbs, we camped together by Mission Creek.

Our camp that evening wasn't anything special. It wasn't a spectacular spot with great views. The sunset wasn't any prettier than the evening before or after. But, it's memorable to me because it was spent with some of my favorite people, including Optimist, Rocketcop and Jeff. We used the opportunity of the cool, well-flowing creek water to wash the dirt off our legs and to launder our clothes for the first time. We were giddy at the thought of washing our belongings and beings. It wasn't entirely productive without soap, but we still managed to slough off layers of dirt, sweat and salt crystals that had accumulated on our few items of clothing.

When it came time to sleep, we realized that Jeff didn't pack a tent. Rocketcop slept in his sleeping bag without a tent, also known as cowboy camping. Optimist and I had our own two-person tent. We planned on setting up our tent and letting Rocketcop and Jeff enjoy the great outdoors the cowboy way.

I am not a fan of cowboy camping. I like the outdoors, but I draw the line on actually sleeping outside. I'm completely vulnerable to any bug, rodent, snake or animal that wants to crawl on me or sniff me while I'm dreaming away and most likely not going to wake up. Though they were thin, I liked my tent walls. It was my little piece of civilization among the wild.

That night, as the sun went down and the only light left was quickly fading from purple into dark blue and black, we noticed visitors over our heads. It was a collection of bats, and it was the only night on the trail that I ever noticed them. Of course, we had to notice them the night that two of the four of us were sleeping in the open air, watching the bats sporadically dip down close to our campsite and our heads. Optimist and I were carefully covered in our two-person tent, watching the bats from inside our mesh roof. I felt a little guilty that we were protected from the bats while Jeff, our "guest" so to speak, was left vulnerable.

As we were falling asleep, we heard Jeff say jokingly, with a hint of honest fear in his voice, "Brother Bear?"

Though Jeff was in his early twenties, he still had the younger brother reverence for Optimist and we could tell that he hoped we'd offer some protection from the bats.

Right then we knew we didn't have it in us to stay tucked inside the tent. If Jeff and Rocketcop had to cowboy camp among the bats, so did we. We abandoned our tent, left our packs inside of it, and fell asleep just a few feet away from Jeff and Rocketcop. The bats were left to flit randomly above our heads. So far as I know, they never touched us, but I slept so soundly that the bats could have carried me across the world and I wouldn't have so much as turned in my sleep.

Though the miles were tough and the bats above our sleeping heads were less than desirable, the added element of Jeff to the group lightened the mood. We were excited to be sharing such an important piece of our lives with someone so close to us. We were showing him first-hand what our lives had been like for the last ten days and what our lives would be like for the next few months. It felt like show and tell day all over again, only a lot harder because the "show" part of the equation involved a lot of walking.

People can say they understand what you go through physically and mentally on the trail (or insert any life experience here), but none can really claim to truly know your situation until they've walked the miles themselves. Having the opportunity for Jeff to join us, even for just over a day, meant a lot to Optimist and me. Living a trail vicariously is certainly meaningful, especially when it's nearly impossible for some people to take on that sort of physical challenge. But when someone can be walking with you, right there at your side, it builds a bond and accurately conveys your lifestyle to them.

It probably shouldn't have mattered to Optimist and I that someone else knew what we were going through, but it in fact still did. It kept up my motivation to keep walking to know that we could share our experience with Jeff and be proud of the choices we were making in hiking the trail. It led me to anticipate what other experiences could be had along the way and shared with others.

Despite never encountering bats again, our hike still had plenty of too-close-for-comfort experiences with other living creatures. Luckily, they were shared with others as well. Also, though I had never really experienced the cliché before, I found out that misery does in fact love company.

When I had my first experience in staying in a shelter, I'm glad I had other thru-hikers there for support. We were in the middle of Washington, in our third straight day of rain, when we came upon Camp Urich, just after mile 2355. It was a log cabin shelter in the middle of nowhere, and to us it was a shining star in an otherwise dreary setting.

After three days of rain, nothing feels dry. Even if certain gear hasn't touched water, it still feels damp and cold. Unrelenting precipitation makes it very hard to stay warm physically and to stay positive mentally. Seeing the shelter at Camp Urich was like seeing an oasis. I wasn't quite sure that it really existed, or that it really would be dry inside. In fact, it was not only real, but also quite dry and very warm inside.

Upon walking into the shelter, we met two other thru-hikers who also stopped there for the evening, Silver and Backtrack.

Once inside, Optimist and I worked quickly to hang our damp gear on the many hooks placed smartly on the walls, all well above the ground and spaced out to allow for maximum usage. The warmth of the shelter's stove immediately warmed us to the core and dried out our gear. We settled in for the night with our new-found friends, Silver and Backtrack, while we sat on the wooden floor and ate our pasta dinner. After spilling a couple of noodles, I heard a warning from Silver and Backtrack about mice coming out to clean up my crumbs. I shrugged off their comment with a light chuckle, thinking they were only teasing me. Still, I made sure to clean up any nibbles of food that happened to fall out of my bowl.

There wasn't electricity in the shelter, and since the windows were small in size and few in number, it was nearly pitch black inside with the darkened gloom of clouds outside. Despite it being early evening, we all stretched out on the floor in our sleeping bags, ready to let sleep take us.

After just a few minutes, I heard the first squeak. It was a noise I had not yet heard on the trail. The other three were familiar with the sound, as they had all hiked the Appalachian Trail. They had spent many nights in the shelters on the AT, where mice regularly set up shop. The one story I remember most vividly about the AT was one of a mouse eating crumbs out of a hiker's beard while he slept. That visual has never left me.

"What was that?" I asked timidly into the dark, hoping it was just my mind that heard it.

I don't remember the exact response I got, but it seemed to be a combination of another squeak and the others breaking out in laughter. Either way, I realized that we were transient residents in a shelter of full-time mice. They no doubt made a good living of feeding off remnants of food that hikers had left behind.

A few more multiple, simultaneous squeaks cut through the dark shelter.

"I've never heard them be so loud!" Optimist chuckled in disbelief. "They usually wait to come out until we at least fall asleep!"

"You weren't kidding? They really exist out here?!" I was half laughing, half crying as I exclaimed into the darkness. Suddenly all the hooks made sense. They weren't just for drying our gear. They were for protecting our food.

I wondered why they didn't seriously warn me earlier, though it wouldn't have changed anything. I certainly wasn't sleeping outside in the rain, and I wouldn't have believed them until I heard my first real squeak.

So it was that I spent my first and last night in a shelter with Optimist, Silver and Backtrack, among the resident mice squeaking and scampering across the floor just inches away from me, in search of crumbs that I most likely left. I was glad to share the experience with others, and even more glad to continue up the trail the next morning, leaving the mice for the next unsuspecting hikers.

There was no shortage of thru-hikers in Southern and Central California as we walked our way north. With around three hundred people attempting the thru-hike on average each year, it feels pretty crowded at the start. Most hikers start in the same time frame due to the seasons. They can't start too early, as they'll reach the snowy sections of Central California too soon, and they can't start too late, as Southern California runs out of water quickly in the oncoming summer heat. As time goes on, people spread out, groups dwindle in numbers, and sections begin to feel downright lonely.

We started late in the season compared with the majority of thru-hikers, so we were at the back of the pack from the beginning. Because we covered more miles on average than the hikers ahead of us, we caught nearly every hiker that started before us. It was actually a great way to meet everyone on the trail. As we made our way north, we saw all the names ahead of us in the trail journals along the way. We knew we were catching people because we found our names getting closer and closer to those signing in ahead of us.

We loved placing faces to the names as we caught up with them, as we never knew what to expect. What kind of faces do you picture when you hear the names Stormin Norman, Hell on Wheels, Reaper, Hot Pants, Salt Lick, etc...? We had no idea either.

Most hikers were easy to pass. We would usually camp with them one night and see them for the last time the next morning. We called ourselves LIFOs, Last In, First Out, because we usually showed up last to camp in the evening and left first in the morning.

Despite it being fun meeting people and catching others almost on a daily basis, it was also difficult to create strong bonds with other hikers early on. So many factors were in play that we rarely saw many people for more than a day or two. There were magnetic towns to stop in, blisters and other injuries held people back, people ran out of money, and honestly, the trail was just too difficult for some to overcome.

The trail, just like Accounting 101 in college, weeded people out pretty quickly. Because of this, the further we moved north, the less thru-hikers there were, and the stronger our bonds became with the hikers that were still around.

A few hikers were more difficult to pass. We leapfrogged with them for a few days until finally one of us stopped in a town and the other gained ground. Achilles, No Car, and Germinator were very difficult to pass.

It wasn't until Northern California, in Belden, where we met No Car, and it just a few days later in Old Station, where we met Achilles and Germinator. To us, it was almost like meeting legends. We had seen their names frequently in the trail journals for the last two months, each day pulling them closer and closer to us. For so long, all of them were just within our reach but never quite close enough for us to catch them. It took each of them stopping in towns for at least a day for us to finally meet them.

To them, we were just two hikers they'd never heard of. They didn't see our excitement in catching them in the same light. It took time for Achilles and No Car to warm up to us. They had been at the front of the pack for most of their hike thus far, and since they weren't looking for anyone new to show up, I don't think they liked the idea of us passing them.

No Car, a Canadian who had quit his ten-year career in commercial real estate to hike the PCT, was a tall, lanky hiker with a booming, froggy voice, eyes the color of ice, and a grizzly beard to show for his time on the trail. He named himself such because he refused to enter a car from Mexico to Canada. It posed difficulties when some towns were miles from the trail, and hitching a ride was the easiest option. Lastly, he was both a gear junkie with all the latest technologically advanced gear, and an attention junkie who loved the spotlight thrown his way.

Achilles was the quietly sarcastic type, and regardless of having a pacemaker put on his twenty-seven-year-old heart just months before hiking, he was a fast hiker and an amazing photographer. He could handle any mileage we threw his way. Despite being the loner type of person who craved time with himself, he warmed up to our company while he kept his distance. Early on in his hike he dealt with Achilles heel pain, and by the time we met him, he too sported a densely grown beard.

Germinator, a pale redhead ironically from Hawaii with a strong depth of knowledge in seemingly everything, was a bit warmer to us from the start. He was doing the trail differently from everyone else, including eating a raw food diet nearly the entire way. I doubt he ever felt threatened from anyone since he'd always gone it alone so confidently his entire life. He saw us as just two more people to talk to, walk with, and camp with.

They were all like three lone wolves who were without a pack, and we provided the company they unknowingly craved. We also provided a way to get in around twenty-five to thirty miles a day. It was the pace we were hiking when we met them and they liked the idea of moving quickly up the trail with us. None of them were going our pace when we caught them, but our mileage certainly fit them once they saw how well it worked for us.

Little did we know that those three would stick around us for nearly six hundred miles.

While Achilles and Germinator were pleased with covering ground with such speed and ease, No Car often complained about the daily mileage. Upon arriving to camp each evening, usually last, he would exclaim, "Can't we hike a mileage that starts with a two and not a three?! And I don't mean twenty-nine point three miles!"

We would simply reply with a big smile and a sarcastic tone, "We're not forcing you to hike with us, but if you want to be around us, this is what we're doing."

He would still mumble mileage complaints under his breath as he set up his tent each evening, but seemed to think our company, along with that of Achilles and Germinator, was worth the extra work. He hiked whatever miles we did each day.

Some of my best memories are from the time we spent with those three, from miles hiked together, to snack breaks, camp time and town time…we shared a lot of good moments together. No Car tended to set up his tent right near the foot of ours, just like a dog sleeps at the foot of its owner's bed. We weren't going to keep him from joining us, but thankfully he eventually gave us more space. Once Achilles started camping with us, also sleeping near our tent, he formed his own club, the Stray Dog Posse, inducting both No Car and him as honorary members.

Germinator never became an official member, as he usually kept his distance and independence. That too fit us just fine. He had his own quirks to speak of, including an involved stretching routine each morning that would challenge any yoga instructor. He put his body in contortions and positions I didn't think possible before sunrise. Achilles even had the pictures to prove it.

Food and friends also went hand-in-hand. Where there was food, there was likely at least one thru-hiker, but more likely a whole group of them. We were like bears: feed us and we'll stick around until the food is gone and we'll likely share the news to other hikers that food is available.

If you think it's fun to share a meal with friends or family in everyday life, think of how greatly that meal and the presence of friends is appreciated when your stomach is achingly hungry and you are bursting at the seams with good stories. I'm not sure which comes first in the mutually beneficial relationship between food and friends, but I do know that one without the other is never really complete.

We were lucky to share many meals, both at camp and in town, with the three lone wolves. While the meals at camp were never grand, nor hardly satisfying for all that I craved, No Car managed to make them fun. Nearly every night, out of boredom, a lack of motivation and pure exhaustion, No Car would resort to Top Ramen for dinner, as it cooked very quickly with very little effort. As we sat around the campfire, watching his paltry homemade stove try to boil water, he would cook his pack of "Noodle Bricks" as he called them, and shuffle through the rest of his stuff sack of food. I'm not sure what he expected to find in it other than the same assortment of noodles, trail mix and energy bars that were there the last time he looked. Regardless, he still pawed through his bag as if better food were going to magically appear, repeating out loud to himself, "What else, what else..."

Then there were the town meals spent together over the likes of pizza and milkshakes all through Northern California and Oregon. Besides my memory bringing back the taste of those first bites of cheese laden, buttery crusted pizza, washed down with a glass of soda and followed up with bowls of ice cream, I most remember the glee on the faces around me. There was often tangible excitement in the air at spending time with new-found friends, and with sharing that time amidst a much-needed meal.

That excitement shone through in a fire in our eyes that was often hard to shake upon being re-energized by food and rest. It was the fire that drove us to keep walking, to keep pushing ourselves mentally and physically, to keep on going because we knew that the experiences we were having both within ourselves and among others were changing our lives forever. We knew a change was happening within us that could not be helped from touching and changing the lives of those around us, including other thru-hikers and our friends and family at home.

I felt that fire so many times along the trail when we were among friends. Even if it was just a simple snack break along the trail, nothing more than a handful of granola or mixed nuts, it was still better shared with friends.

No Car, Achilles and Germinator were a big part of most of the second half of our hike. We were sad when we parted ways with each of them one by one, first Germinator early on in Oregon, then Achilles much later in Oregon, and finally No Car on the Oregon/Washington border. Like Rocketcop, they all finished the trail, just not with us. It was a mutually beneficial relationship across the board with them, as No Car said that at one point he was feeling so alone that he "danced with his shadow." Optimist and I were thankful for their presence in our lives along the trail, for it would have never been the same, and would have possibly not been as good, had we not shared so much time with them.

It was nearly impossible *not* to share the trail with others. Others were inevitably out there. Though we could go hours or even days without so much hearing a twig snap under the weight of another hiker's foot, we never felt alone. Even if I had not had Optimist, I would have felt surrounded and supported by other people. The trail is an individual experience in that only you can put on your pack, pick up your feet, and walk. No one else is going to walk the miles for you.

At the same time, the trail is very much a communal experience. The sum of all the individual experiences happening in the same bubble together forms a petri dish of a community that thrives on itself. Long-distance backpacking has its own underground culture full of lingo, etiquette, and even celebrities. Trail journals, for example, are just one piece of that culture that helps create such a tightly knit community.

On the trail, there is a constant balance between the individual and communal experience. You want what is best for yourself, what is going to give you the best odds of succeeding. Yet, you are also part of a greater group that is moving as one small mass from Mexico to Canada. Though your legs are doing the walking, the support of others and the knowledge that others are walking the same difficult miles is what helps you get through the miles after all. This is no different from life off the trail.

As Rocketcop says, "It's all about the experience," and other people are part of that experience, for better or for worse. They will not be shut out. Other people cannot be avoided or cut out entirely, so rather than try and cut them out, we should find a way to enjoy their presence. At the very least, it's a matter of learning how to share life with others.

It's nearly impossible to avoid other people in life, much less not count on others to fulfill some sort of need. Mentally walk yourself through your day and try and count the number of people that make your daily life possible, including the electricity you use, the coffee you drink, the roads you drive...You could not begin to know just how many people have played a part in your day, and you surely could not do life alone. If we all tried, it would be mighty hard, and if we succeeded, who would be there to celebrate that feat with us if the whole point was to cut people out?

Though it's difficult, it is attainable to embrace other's presence while at the same time maintain the fire within us. There is a delicate balance to maintain, to keep one's independence from the group, to uphold one's identity, at the same time of sharing as a community and adding to the petri dish so it keeps thriving. We can be independent of others, knowing at the same time that we are that much better as a sum of all the parts rather than all the parts standing separately.

Despite these realizations, I still struggle with my own connections with others on a daily basis, often cutting the cord before I've made enough effort to truly string together a bond. I make excuses of why my schedule and my time do not allow me to stop and grow moss on the rocks of my relationships with others. I am too busy, I'd rather do it alone, it's too complicated...the list goes on of why I do not allow many others to share in my life.

Oftentimes, I find myself thinking, "I love humanity as an idea, but on a one on one basis, I can't stand people."

This mindset often leaves me cursing humanity as I snip the poorly woven threads of my relationships with others. I have a very difficult time adding to the community in my everyday life, too scared that my individual identity will be forfeited, or too impatient with others' idiosyncrasies to be as forgiving of them as they are of me. After all, I'm probably just as hard to get along with others as they are to me.

It is at these moments, when I am honest with the fact that others have to make efforts to enjoy my presence just the same as I do, I step back from myself. I remember that the sum of all my life experiences would have never been possible had it not been for the involvement of others in my life. I am responsible for carrying my own weight and moving my own feet, but others have always been there with me, cheering me on and encouraging me to live my life to my own expectations. Without others, including Optimist and my family, I may have never started nor overcome many of my life's challenges, whether self-imposed or circumstantial. There is not a thing I would change about how their presence has served me thus far, so I cannot imagine untying the knots that have so far strengthened me. It is the new knots that also need work and attention.

Life happens, whether we are ready for it or not. Failure and success happen. People exist outside of ourselves, whether we want them to or not. Given these factors out of our control, life's ups are more fully enjoyed and life's downs are more easily bounced back from among the presence of friends, family and even complete strangers.

6 ANGELS AND DEMONS DO EXIST

Trail angels that is. People who, planfully or spontaneously, greatly enhance the lives of thru-hikers through acts of selfless kindness. Any form of help that someone gives to hikers is known as trail magic, and those performing it are known as trail angels. Trail angels perform acts of trail magic on a varied scale, from simple to astounding. They leave coolers along the side of the trail full of water, soda, and sometimes beer, they pick up hikers off the side of a road and drive them into town, and they even open up their homes and therefore laundry machines, showers and beds to hikers. There is no limit to the selflessness of trail angels. They unconditionally give to hikers what goes beyond holding the door open for you, beyond normal humanity, beyond anything a thank-you card can cover.

The first seven hundred miles of the trail were tough because of the lack of water, but it would have been much, much harder had there not been trail angels who supplied hikers with gallons of water and coolers of beverages during most of the driest sections. We often found coolers or stashes of water jugs tucked behind rocks, under bushes, or right off the side of the trail in more remote locations. When heavy coolers or equally heavy jugs of water were seemingly in the middle of nowhere, I often thought, "Who in the world would come out here just to leave water for us?"

A trail angel, that's who.

Just like those coolers full of thirst-quenching drinks, there were countless other coolers that flash across my mind in thinking about trail angels. The one in Central California that was loaded with mini-chocolate bars in an assortment of flavors. I took one of each kind, savoring each as it melted on my tongue, careful to make the flavor last. There was the box of fresh plums, the cooler of fresh apricots, and the tin of energy bars, grapefruit and water, all in separate spots in Northern California. An assortment of Gatorades was strewn in a pile on a random logging road in Oregon, miles from any sort of civilization. Most memorable was the cooler with Sprite and Snickers bars which we unknowingly passed. I would have never enjoyed that glorious bar of chocolate, caramel and nuts had Achilles not been sitting just past it, quick to chide us as he gazed past our shoulders at the tucked away cooler, "What would you guys do without me?"

I swear it tasted better knowing that I almost missed out on it.

When we came upon a bit of trail magic, in the shape of jugs of water or coolers of unfathomably good food and drink, I always wished the trail angel could have been there. I wanted to thank each trail angel for what they did for my experience. Their acts could lift me out of a crappy day, a day that I didn't want to walk or even be outside, a day where I just wanted to cash in my chips for creature comforts, a day where I was questioning every part of my life and every motivation for each of my actions. They were part of the reason I ever made it through to the end.

Even more amazing than the trail angels who sprinkled stashes of food and drink up and down the trail were the "established" trail angels. This kind of trail angel gives out their phone numbers and offers up their hospitality to all thru-hikers. Some are so established that their information is in guidebooks. Imagine having your name, phone number and address published in a book, telling people you have an open-door policy, no appointment necessary. That is one dedicated trail angel.

The most established trail angel we visited was Hiker Heaven in Southern California. It was truly an amazing setup. Though it's simply someone's home that they've opened up to hikers, it really is an oasis, and it really is heavenly.

Hiker Heaven offered not only amenities to thru-hikers, but it was also well-organized and downright professional in its execution of trail magic. There was literally a road map for the "menu" of trail magic being offered. Just inside the garage were instructions posted on a board, the tri-fold kind you see at science fairs in school. Directions instructed thru-hikers to a tent of spare clothing, a sign-up sheet for showers, and a laundry basket with name tags for dirty clothes.

In addition to those already amazing offerings, Hiker Heaven had a car for hikers to drive to Los Angeles for resupplies, huge tents set up for sleeping, and a laptop with internet access. And it's all run by one family that has an undeniable love for hikers. How else could they handle up to three hundred people visiting their home every summer if they didn't at least have a fancy for thru-hikers?

The only bad thing about Hiker Heaven is that you don't want to leave. When we went through, there were many others who had just arrived, who were leaving soon, or who had been there too long and didn't look like they'd be hitting the trail anytime soon. Why leave such an oasis for more hard miles on the trail? It's a question that I later found out many couldn't answer.

Hiker Heaven is just an example of one of the many established trail angels along the way. Many other trail angels offer up their home, their energy, and inadvertently their money, in order to make many thru-hikers' experiences that much better. We didn't visit every trail angel along the way, but still managed to enjoy the places we did visit. Trail angels made up some of the best parts of the trail for Optimist and me. They made my hike all the more enjoyable and easier, two feats that are by no means small.

Perhaps the coolest thing about trail angels is that all the previously described acts of trail magic are the norm. Not that it is expected that people will leave jugs of water, give rides into town, or open their homes for strangers' use. These are simply acts that most thru-hikers experience. Yes, the trail magic is still special, but everyone revels in it just the same. The real excitement and awe lies in the trail magic that occurs when it's least expected, when it's beyond a cold drink or a free ride, when you believe that people really are innately good after all.

Optimist and I were especially lucky in receiving trail magic. We were lathered in trail magic from day one all the way to the end, benefiting not only from the established trail angels, but also the spontaneous ones. This kind of angel was a person so moved by our journey that they became a trail angel after meeting us. It was the spontaneous ones that molded our personal trail magic. Our brand of trail magic was one-of-a-kind, limited edition, while supplies last, and we took advantage of every moment of it.

One trait of trail angels was how willing they were to offer up their own possessions to us and other thru-hikers. I certainly don't find myself freely offering up my stuff to just any old stranger, or friend for that matter. The selflessness of trail angels seems to be on a whole different level than most.

There was a morning in Central California where the trail followed the highway for a brief stint before it returned to natural ground. It had been a tiring morning. We started the day with a big uphill climb, and it wasn't getting any easier. It was the kind of climb where you can see someone ahead of you as a mere speck, high up in the distance. You know you must somehow get to that point as well, and it's not by cruising on flat ground.

That day, we planned on stopping for food at the Echo Lake's General Store. All I had in mind was ice cream, and all I knew was that I had a lot of walking to do before we reached it. Once we left the road and reached the trail again, we found ourselves in a parking lot at the trailhead.

A middle-aged couple, most likely day hikers, was looking at the map posted at the trailhead.

Their faces were full of confusion and concern. They looked like they were in pretty good physical shape, but didn't look like seasoned outdoors people. They saw us making our way across the parking lot towards the trail, and quickly asked us, "Is this the PCT?"

We *were* the perfect ones to ask. It was the only trail we were concerned with finding.

"Yep, this is the trailhead. Just follow this trail and you're on the PCT," Optimist happily answered.

"You guys look like you've been out here for a while. Where are you coming from?" They had stopped looking at the map and focused their attention on us.

"Mexico! We're thru-hiking the trail," Optimist answered even more happily.

"Wow! That's amazing!" They exclaimed in unison.

Now they were really eying us up and down. They probably hadn't met many people coming from Mexico, as this looked like their first time on the trail at all.

After we explained a little more about our adventure, along with how long we'd been outside, and how much further we had to go, they asked, "Well…do you need anything? Are you hungry?"

I turned to Optimist, both of us trying to contain our grins. We knew that the most dangerous question to ask a thru-hiker was if they were hungry, because the answer was always, inevitably, without a doubt, "Yes!"

I'm sure they could read it in our eyes or just look at our small frames. Before we answered, the woman opened up their SUV's trunk and starting pulling out grocery bags of food.

"Let's see, we've got potato chips, soda, salami, cheese and crackers…here, take whatever you want."

She wouldn't stop pulling out items from paper bags and a cooler.

We couldn't resist the temptation and broke down and accepted their offer. Optimist took the cheese and crackers and I mixed the salty, oily goodness of Lay's chips with Diet Pepsi. I loved feeling the carbonation bubble up in my throat.

It was pure joy, standing there in the parking lot with complete strangers as we nearly inhaled the food. I tried to be polite and eat slowly, but felt hurried because I knew we must part with them and their trunk of food at some point.

As we ate, we talked with the couple about the trail, learned where they were from and shared a couple of our stories. It felt so natural, standing there at the back of their car, chatting with our new-found trail angels and eating their food. Still, Optimist and I didn't want to out-stay our welcome, so we parted ways before they regretted helping us. I left with a renewed sense of energy and a pocket full of caramel candies, touched by the goodness and sincerity of such spontaneous trail angels.

Countless times during our journey, trail angels appeared when we weren't even paying attention, or when we weren't wishing for trail magic to pull us out of a slump. The Central California portion of the trail ends in the town of Belden. The town lies at one of the lowest elevations along the entire trail, and one quickly learns that a town low in elevation means one must come down from the mountain somehow.

It was a rather hellish descent into the town through thick bushes laden with poison oak. The temperature got warmer and the air more humid with every foot of elevation lost. Optimist and I made the best of the descent. We stayed positive despite the hot sun and elevated temperatures, happy to be reaching a town early that afternoon. Once we reached the Belden Town Resort, we found that the resort was one large building broken down into several shops. Unfortunately, everything was closed and not a single sign of life was present. We were shocked and a little worried to find it closed. We had planned on at least eating a good meal there.

We passed the empty building and made our way up the road, towards the rest of the town. As we were walking, an ice cream truck passed us, heading toward the deserted building. The driver also found that it was closed, turned around, and drove back down the road on which we were walking. We saw the truck stop about fifty yards ahead of us. The driver got out and talked briefly to a guy who was standing out by the road in front of his home. We saw the driver hand something to the guy and point back to us. We were a bit confused and unsure why he'd be pointing at us, and didn't want to get too excited about the possibility of ice cream. Up until that point, we'd done nothing other than daydream of spending the afternoon in the back of his truck.

When we walked up to the stranger, who was still standing near the road, he was enjoying a Butterfinger ice cream bar. He tossed one to each of us and said, "Here you go; these are from the driver. He thought you might want these. Better eat 'em quick though; they're starting to melt."

We couldn't believe it. As we unwrapped the bars, we were still in shock from such a random act of kindness. The driver had only briefly glanced at us as he drove by us, hadn't asked for a thing in return, and had stopped just to give us free ice cream.

We stood there with the stranger, all three of us eating our blissful ice cream bars among few spoken words. Optimist and I were also trying to solve our previous problem of the shops being closed. Luckily, we had the phone number of the established trail angels that lived in town, so we decided to call them. Optimist dug through his pack for the scribbled phone number, but it was no use after he found it. Our cell phone didn't have service.

At that point two motorcyclists drove up next to us. They had also found the shops closed and wanted to ask us about them. It seemed the shop owners had underestimated their amount of business.

When the two motorcyclists heard we also needed to reach a store, but that our phone didn't have service, one of them didn't hesitate to pull out his cell phone and offer it up to us. We graciously used it, careful to not waste minutes, and were soon picked up off the trail by the town's official trail angels. They drove us to the local café where we met up with other thru-hikers and basked in the atmosphere of milkshakes and french fries. Later that day we spent the hottest part of the day in the cool shade of the trail angel's home, filling ourselves with freshly baked peanut butter cookies from the their kitchen.

We were on a conveyor belt of trail angels that day, being passed from one to the next. Gloves donned, or course. We were quite dirty at that point.

There were plenty more random acts of kindness directed towards us from trail angels along the way. In every instance, there was a complete lack of selfishness towards sharing possessions with us, especially food and water, the life-lines on the trail. People who may have had no intentions of giving food away to other hikers were instantly moved to help us. Maybe we looked that hungry, maybe we were always in the right place at the right time, or maybe people really are good to the core. They just need the chance to show that goodness.

Ninety-nine percent of the people we met on the trail were good people, and lots of them were trail angels, whether they gave us something as simple as a good conversation over a warm campfire for the evening, or something as grand as our own cabin for the night.

There is always the one percent who ruins the party for the other ninety-nine percent who work so hard to put it together. That one percent represents the one demon, the one bad apple that we had the misfortune of crossing paths with along the trail.

Optimist and I were in Southern Oregon. We planned on having lunch at the next water source along the trail, which happened to be one of the many lakes we passed in Oregon. We eyed the perfect lunch spot just a few feet from the trail. It was a flat, cleared area surrounded by trees lying on the ground in a circle, creating the perfect benches. About fifty feet away was an RV parked and a large black, muscular dog chained to its outside, barking relentlessly upon our arrival. The dog's owner sat just inside the doorway, making it difficult to see his face. After eying us for a moment he stood up slowly and lumbered out of the doorway, yelling at the dog to shut up.

That should have been our first hint to just keep walking in hopes of a better lunch spot. We had yet to meet someone that couldn't at least tolerate us politely, so we said a quick hello to him above the dog's barking, and proceeded to unpack our food for lunch. The man, dressed in a tan sweatshirt and camouflage cargo pants, didn't respond and simply stared out from under the stiff brim of his hat.

We needed water to cook, and the only path that could reach the lake went fairly close to the man's RV. Optimist started walking towards it anyway. The only other way to the lake was through marshy reeds that promised mucky water. As soon as Optimist made his way to the water, the man grumbled loudly, "Why do you have to get water here?"

Optimist, surprised by the man's question, stopped and said, "Well, this is the only good path to the water."

"Well, there's plenty of lake over there!" The man yelled as he pointed off into the distance of the lake. He obviously meant *way* over there.

"Yeah, but this is the only good path to the water. I just need to fill my bottles so we can eat lunch."

As Optimist starting walking toward the water, the man yelled (meanwhile the dog is barking this entire time), "Why the hell can't you mind your own business?"

"Huh?" Optimist said.

Neither of us knew why he was so angry. We had obviously missed some piece of the puzzle.

"Huh?" he repeated, mocking Optimist.

Optimist paused for a second, contemplating how far he should chance pushing the man and his dog, and headed back towards me, empty bottles in hand.

"That's fine. I'll just get water somewhere else," Optimist said over his shoulder as he walked away. I was glad he didn't push the man further, as he looked ready to snap and equally ready to unleash his dog.

We packed up our stuff without skipping a beat. His dog continued to snarl his teeth at us, and the man's eyes never lifted their harsh gaze from our movements. We walked on for another twenty minutes and found a remote spot for lunch on the bank of the same lake.

It was a quiet lunch. We were in shock from our first negative encounter with a stranger.

We later found out from Achilles that he had stopped at the same spot for breakfast just a few hours before us. He had been eating his bowl of granola and rehydrated milk at the mouth of the lake when the man emerged from his RV, angered at finding someone just outside his doorway, and equally eager to kick Achilles out. Achilles had woken the bear and we'd annoyed it even further. I'm sure several other hikers followed after us that day, making the same mistake to settle down for a break, only to find that they weren't welcome in a public place.

The incident left a sour taste in my mouth for quite some time that day. It wasn't that the man was a complete jerk to us. It wasn't that we had to delay our lunch and find a different spot further down the trail.

It was that he felt that he owned a part of the land, that he selfishly hovered over and laid claim to not only the spot on which he parked his RV, but also the only entry point into the lake and the other camping sites surrounding his own. He was on public land just off a national scenic trail, yet he carried the air that we had no right to be there, that we were intruding on his property.

We had called the trail our home for over seventy days at that point, never claiming to own even a speck of dirt or a handful of rocks. We felt that we were transient residents of a world that could never be owned, that would always be wild, and which would always outlive our existence.

I was angry with the man all day until I reasoned that there must be some reason, that there must have been some trauma in his life, to make him want to be in control of everything, right down to the land and water that surrounded him. It made me sad to think of how disillusioned he must have been to think that he could truly own a piece of land or the mouth of a lake and keep it away from others to enjoy as a temporary piece of their own happiness. It also made me realize how silly we must all be to think that we can actually *own* land and lay claim to controlling everything that occurs on it. These were quite shocking realizations to have after such a blunt meeting with the one demon along the trail.

Optimist and I were lucky that we only had one trail demon among all the other angels. The acts of the trail angels greatly outweighed the brief encounter with the demon man and his demon dog. They simply made trail angels that much more special.

Putting aside the water caches, the coolers, the spontaneous acts of kindness, and the one demon along the way, there existed legendary trail magic that Optimist and I received on our journey that went beyond any previous stories of trail magic we had ever heard. We can hardly believe our own stories today because they are acts of kindness that just don't happen often on the trail, and definitely never happen in real life. They are stories of complete strangers helping us out with no strings attached, unconditional support simply because we were out hiking a trail, and they connected with us on some level of our lifestyle.

While in Southern Oregon, we stopped at the Hyatt Lake Resort. It wasn't much of a resort, but it had two important ingredients: pizza and ice cream. We could not pass it up.

After we finished eating, we packed up our stuff on the picnic benches outside the restaurant and chatted with the other pizza patrons about our hike.

They were asking the typical questions, like what do we eat, what do we carry, how many miles do we hike each day. With each answer we gave, their faces carried the shock value we knew we could always produce.

It was almost time for us to leave when a man walked up to us who had been sitting outside with his family as well. He hadn't been asking us questions, but I doubt it was easy for him to ignore us as he and his family sat within ear shot of our conversation with the others. He asked us where we were going to stay that night, and we said simply, "I don't know, somewhere off the side of the trail."

It was the absolute truth. We never really had a true plan of where we stayed on any given day. Too many factors threatened to crush well-laid plans, so we only ventured to pencil them in, declaring our home as somewhere off the side of the trail.

He proceeded to tell us that his family had two vacation cabins just down the road on Hyatt Lake; one was empty. He then asked if we would like to stay in the empty one for the night, our jaws dropping as we heard his generous offer. Would we like to stay in a vacation cabin, on a lake, in a bed, with a hot shower and laundry? YES!

After the initial shock of the offer, we quickly accepted and he dropped us off at the empty cabin, promising that he and his family would return to their cabin after eating dinner.

It was one of the most memorable nights on the trail. That evening they drove us to a fire tower to watch the sunset, and we could see Crater Lake off in the distance, one of our next destinations. Later that evening, while our clean clothes tumbled in the dryer, they made a bonfire and we sat outside in a circle of lawn chairs. We talked for hours and passed a tin of chocolate-covered almonds around our circle. Optimist and I even stayed up late watching movies and basking in the paradise of our own cabin. To top it off, they woke up early to make us a breakfast spread of waffles with homemade jam, syrup, quiche and coffee. It was trail magic of legendary status, a story of complete strangers spontaneously rising to the occasion to become some of our best trail angels.

As if that wasn't enough, three days later, we reached Crater Lake. In the data book, it indicated we could send mail boxes to the Crater

Lake Lodge, which was nearly right on the trail. It also said there were meals and groceries at the Crater Lake Lodge. Along with sending ourselves a large resupply box of food, we gave the address to our friends and family, so there was a possibility of us receiving several care packages.

Many other hikers stopped seven miles short of Crater Lake that day at the Mazama Campground. There was an all-you-can-eat buffet, but we passed the campground because we were hopeful for what was awaiting us at the lodge instead.

We had to walk twenty-eight miles to get to Crater Lake that day, and needed to arrive by 5:00 p.m. to make sure stores would still be open. That in itself was no small feat.

We first arrived at the small café and souvenir shop located a few minutes away from the lodge and thought to ourselves, "I really hope this isn't the 'Meals and Groceries' mentioned in the book." There were no groceries other than candy bars, and the meals were expensive, small-portioned, ready-made salads and sandwiches.

We shrugged off the lack of meals and groceries and made our way to the lodge where our packages were awaiting us. Unfortunately, we were told that the address listed in the book was incorrect. A phone call by the lodge's manager to the Mazama Campground discovered that our packages were all at the campground, seven miles back. Seven miles down the difficult climb we had just overcome. To top it off, there was no public transportation between the lodge and the campground.

Even worse in the bleak picture was that I had sent myself new shoes in our box of food, and desperately needed them. Duct tape was holding up the soles of my hiking boots at the time. I had already squeezed 1300 miles out of the shoes and didn't want to risk asking more of them.

Suddenly things were looking really, really bad as we stood in the lodge's entryway, weighing our options. We also caught a whiff of our body odor and realized that we should sit outside and contemplate what to do, rather than receive funny looks from the employees and guests while we stood in the lobby.

While we were sitting outside in front of the lodge, about thirty cyclists rode up. They all lined up their bikes and were getting ready to go into the lodge. We talked with a few of them about what they were doing and found out they were all part of a group cyclist tour of Oregon. We told them we were thru-hiking the PCT and answered a few questions on both sides of the conversation. We had only been chatting with a few of them for five minutes or so, when a couple that was part of the group, with whom we'd only exchanged a few words with, approached us and politely asked, "What would you say if we bought you two a room at the lodge for the night?"

It was another jaw-dropping moment. Complete strangers were offering to pay for a room at the lodge. It was our ticket to creature comforts for the evening, and their only motivation was to make sure we used it. We'd already looked at the prices of the rooms, so we knew the enormity of the gift they were offering. Though we felt guilty accepting the free room, the pull of how tired, dirty and hungry we were was too much, and we had yet to come up with a plan B. We accepted, still shocked at the generous offer. While the husband was checking us into a room, I talked with his wife. She recounted a hiking trip she took with her daughter in Spain. They too would arrive dirty and smelly to hotels along the way and would be snuffed by the hotel employees. The employees acted like she and her daughter couldn't afford a room based on how they appeared. She knew how we were feeling, how badly we needed a shower and a bed, and how we felt walking into a hotel lobby with our weather-worn gear and the evident lack of hygiene.

The most amazing thing about these trail angels, as it was with all trail angels we met, was that they wanted nothing in return. Their generosity was completely unconditional. When we offered to buy them a drink at the hotel bar, they resisted, saying they just wanted us to enjoy ourselves at the lodge and indulge in everyday comforts. To cap it off, since we were hotel guests, the employee shuttle that went from the Mazama Campground to the lodge delivered our five packages from our family and friends right to our room. I wasted no time in pouring the contents of each box on our bed. I even took a picture of my new pair of shoes and the pile of boxes. That's how happy I was to see them.

I have done no justice in acknowledging all the trail angels that helped us make it from Mexico to Canada. I can already think of one friend, Rob, who drove us around Los Angeles to find a cure for my golf ball-sized blisters. We eventually did, and my feet were most thankful. Then there was our friend's mother in Central Washington, who opened up her home to us with only the knowledge that we were friends of her son. She didn't know us any better than the next strangers, but she drove forty-five minutes each way to pick us up from the trail, treated us to a night in her home, and trucked us around Issaquah, Washington, to help us buy food and groceries.

Hopefully this chapter at least serves as a humble, small thank you to all the trail angels out there that help hikers along the way. They showed us that maybe people are innately good after all, that maybe there just aren't many ways to express that goodness in everyday life.

While there was no limit to the kindness of trail angels along the trail, it seems hard to translate that to real life. Trail magic isn't commonplace outside of the trail. It really is true that, "You're not in Kansas anymore," once you step off the trail and onto the treadmill of real life. People simply aren't that nice to strangers or even to people they know closely.

What was the last random act of kindness that you gave or received? Did you surprise yourself with the amount of good that you could spread? Were you shocked when someone did a favor for you, without so much as a request from you? Or, were you so shocked when you received that favor that you questioned the motivation of the giver so much that you didn't even enjoy the gift?

It might seem downright weird if a stranger helps you on the street, like that person wants something in return other than just the feeling of making someone's day a bit better. We never stop to consider that maybe that person is just good to the core and enjoys helping another person. I know that I didn't truly believe that could be the case until I met all the angels lining the trail. We seem to have no issues believing that demons exist in our everyday world. Just watch the evening news. What's so hard about believing that angels are among us as well?

I myself am guilty of missing opportunities to be an angel for someone, whether by choice or circumstance. I get so tightly wound in my own ball of yarn that I forget there are others around me. I make excuses for not being kind to others, usually citing the lack of time or energy. It also becomes harder to bring to light those opportunities to spread trail magic in real life. Trail angels know exactly what hikers want: food, showers, laundry, and sleep. The chances to give to others aren't as cut and dry off the trail, which takes that much more effort to bring them to life.

Either way, self-imposed or not, in today's world, it's downright hard to be good. Being civil is one thing. To go beyond the imposed laws that dictate how we act is where the magic happens. Those are the acts that take more energy, more effort, and more caring beyond not breaking the man-made laws. They are also the acts that are worth every ounce of effort once you see the happiness they bring to another human being. Being good to strangers is especially hard. We are taught to rely only on ourselves, to trust no one, and to show no vulnerability.

Disobeying those three principles is what allowed Optimist and me to receive so much trail magic along the way. We openly accepted help from others, we trusted greatly in them, and our physical appearance gave away our vulnerability in an instant. While these aren't exactly admirable traits to have in life, a balancing act of each of them just might break down the barriers we hold up against other people.

I am not saying that we all need to go pick up the homeless person we see on the street corner each afternoon. But, there are plenty of opportunities surrounding us each day that we either don't see or blatantly ignore, that would lend themselves to each of us being an angel in some sort of capacity. No matter how big or small, one never knows the impact an act could have on the person receiving the magic. The opportunities might not be as glorious as a spare vacation cabin, but that is not something we all need in our everyday lives. We need simple acts of unconditional, no strings attached, just for the heck of it, because it feels right, kindness. We are all possible trail angels, and there is no limit to the magic that can happen.

7 COME TO YOUR SENSES

One of the most commonly asked questions I'm asked about the trail is, "What was your favorite part of the trail?"

I never have an answer. It's like asking a parent what kid they like the most. Though they may have a preference (admit it Mom, I'm your favorite), they simply can't give a straightforward answer. There are just too many things that are unique about each child. Each one is loved differently, yet all the same.

It was the same with each section of the trail, each national park that we traversed through, and each state whose border we crossed. The trail was constantly changing as we made our way north. It changed in climate, in terrain, and in other people. Aside from the surroundings, all the while I too was changing on the inside. There is no way a push pin on the map could mark the pinnacle of my experience.

While I enjoyed some sections over others, whether because of great weather, beautiful views or easy hiking, it's simply too difficult to name a favorite. If I had ever reached my favorite spot, I may not have continued hiking. With that thought, maybe Canada was my favorite place, because that was where we stopped walking.

However, every part of me knows that isn't true. All the pieces of the trail are my favorite because of the memories they bring forth and the sensory experiences I have upon remembering them.

Each memory is a sensory experience every time I look back on the trail. Every time I think of a different section of the trail, oftentimes I remember exactly what park we walked through, what lake we slept near, what town the trail scooted by, and even what meals we ate at the time. Those memories then lead me to once again see the deep blue skies and pristine lakes, to smell the wild flowers and onions, to hear the bushes rustle with movement, to taste the huckleberries and blackberries, and to rub the salt-laden straps of my hiking poles between my thumbs and forefingers.

I can't have a memory of the trail without my senses being revived, and I often have sensory experiences in the present that bring me back to the same moment on the trail. It doesn't take much to trigger a memory. Sometimes it's as simple as hearing the words, "ramen noodles." I'm immediately shot back into the mornings in Southern California, when Top Ramen was our breakfast of choice. It cooked quickly and was warm, salty and filling. I can see myself sitting on a tree log, hunched over in soreness from the prior day's hike. As I cup my pot of breakfast between my hands, I feel the ridges on the underside of the metal bowl with my fingertips. I blow on the steamy bowl of noodles to cool it while I stare out into the mountains in anticipation of another day's hike. The steam from the noodles rises to my face, leaving a slight trace of condensation. I can feel the temperature rising with the morning sun, burning off any remaining patches of fog. All these memories flood my mind with the simple mention of ramen noodles.

Sensory experiences from the trail hit me at all times of the day, in every possible situation. There is a running trail just a few minutes from my home, and I run on it nearly every day. Though it's mostly shaded and lined with trees, the trail runs through a short section, lasting about a hundred meters, of an open field with huge power lines running overhead and off into the distance. The power lines are completely out of place along the trail, but people do need their electricity somehow.

If it's quiet enough outside, I can hear the power lines crackle and hum with electricity. As I run underneath them, both the sight and the sound of them takes me back mentally for a brief moment to the days we hiked in central Washington. The scenes from those days repeat in my mind and I can't help from watching them over and over again.

There was one day in particular where we were near the end of a long day of hiking. The trail passed in and out of heavily-wooded sections and clear-cut sections with huge power lines running overhead and sweeping down into the distance. I was a little scared as we scurried underneath the buzzing lines of electricity, the sound being foreign to our ears at the time. The power lines were so powerful and intimidating that I had a fear they might snap and crash down on us. Their presence and sound were so out of place with the lifestyle we'd lived for the last few months. We had not used electricity on a regular basis for over three months, nor had I heard its unmistakable sound.

Since we hadn't relied on electricity to live, we simply didn't have crackling and buzzing as a regular sound during the day. You may think you do not either, but sit still for just a moment in your home, with a light on, the refrigerator running, and the computer humming, and you will realize how accustomed your ears are to these everyday background noises.

The simple, short-lived memory of the power lines often leads to other memories of events that occurred in the same time period. As we made our way through Washington, we were lucky in hitting the berry season just right. The huckleberries were aplenty and ripe for the quick picking. Optimist would fill a plastic bag worth of berries so he could easily snack on them while still maintaining a brisk stride up the trail. My method was to take swipes of the bushes lining the trail, grabbing a fistful at a time, aiming at never breaking stride. We ate so many huckleberries in Washington that our tongues, teeth and palms were stained shockingly blue for the few days that we walked through the berry-filled section. I can't eat a huckleberry, much less a blueberry, without picturing our blue-stained palms outstretched for more and Optimist's blue-tinted lips, teeth and gums grinning widely.

In my daily life, when I'm really motivated, I run on that same trail early in the mornings, just as the sun is coming up. I can't help but place myself on the trail yet again, this time waking up in a cold tent, huddled in my sleeping bag next to Optimist, not wanting to get up but knowing that a beautiful morning and even more beautiful trail is awaiting me.

I admit it, I'm a bed monster. I hit the snooze button at least four times before finally giving in and getting up. Even then, I still complain about how much more I want to sleep. But the mornings I appreciate the most are those where I don't obey that instinct to simply roll over and I head out to the trail for my own morning time.

There is something about the early morning that's simply more hopeful. The entire day lies ahead and everything feels like it's all up to me to decide what path the day takes. There's a calmness, a coolness, and a quietness that comes with the morning hours. Being awake during those hours allows me to contemplate my day and be excited for the fresh start once again.

It was like that most mornings on the trail. The stillness surrounding us was unmatched. There were no cars heard in the distance, no neighborhood dogs barking, and no trains adding to the background noise. The only noises we heard were the ones we made as we unzipped our sleeping bags and our tent, and gathered up our things from the prior evening. The sounds we made pierced the stillness as if the earth woke up just for us to have another day of life.

Optimist and I liked hiking alone most mornings, spending time with our own thoughts before the rest of the trail woke up. Having our mornings to ourselves, and more importantly, our day, was an aspect of the long-distance trail life that most people are never lucky enough to experience. So many of us spend our waking hours, especially the first few, contemplating what needs to be crossed off the list and what fires need to be put out, before the day can really begin. Oftentimes this doesn't allow our minds to spend quality time alone.

It's amazing that there can be so many memories attached to something as simple as the subtle buzz of a power line or the stillness of the early morning. These are connections that I cannot shut out, that I cannot turn off. I cannot stop my mind from taking a mental journey every time I'm reminded of an aspect along the trail, nor would I want to. I love that I can take a thousand mental journeys back to the trail without even a hint to those around me that I've temporarily stepped out of the present for a brief mental moment from the past. My sensory experiences are all my own to have and to remember. The trail was responsible for both creating those memories and strengthening my senses in order to have them.

If there is ever a great injustice that our urban environment imposes on us, it is that it doesn't allow us to truly use our senses. I had never *really* used my senses of smell or hearing before the trail. Both my senses of sight and taste changed because of what was being fed to them, and my sense of touch became a bit muddled because of all the dirt and sweat layered on my body.

A result of the trail that I was completely unprepared for was the strengthening of my senses as we walked. Though I never developed senses that matched any comparison to a wild animal's senses, I stepped out of my human range in order to live more like the trail's full-time residents.

It was in Central California that Optimist and I first smelled wild onions growing near the side of the trail. After smelling them once, we immediately recognized their scent each time they were within fifteen feet of the trail. We would catch their scent and run off the side of the trail, gather a small bunch of them, and later add them to our pot of food. The natural addition of flavor enhanced our meals, though the addition of bad breath was a bit of a downer. We later began to smell food so well that it was almost to our detriment. We could smell a campsite full of food well before we saw it. The delicious smell of cooked food made it difficult *not* to linger at other people's campsites. I began to know how the bears felt about camper's food, and I couldn't blame them for obeying such natural instincts as following their noses and listening to their growling stomachs.

Besides picking up on the oftentimes-irresistible scent of other campers' food, I literally followed the other hikers' marks that they left on the trail. Early on in the trail, after I'd been named Stopwatch, I mentally gave myself the middle name Tracker. I always knew whom we were following by studying the footprints in front of me. Whenever we camped with others, passed others, or simply met them for a brief chat, I'd be sure to memorize the patterns on the bottom of their shoes so I would know who was around us. I would literally ask them to show me the bottoms of their shoes. Several shoes were common on the trail among the thru-hikers, and since I knew those tracks so well, it was easy to know what the people ahead of us were wearing. It only became difficult in times where pine needles were plentiful or when mud altered the tracks.

My sense of hearing heightened along the trail in that I found it easier to judge the size of creatures by the sounds of the rustling along the way. The first few days along the trail were the most nerve-wracking of all. I was so terrified of running into a cougar, a bear or a rattlesnake, that every little rustle in the bushes next to me sent my heart racing and my breathing uneven. It usually ended up being a lizard, a bird or a rabbit, but there was no telling those first few days. I let my imagination run wild as I repeated the aforementioned advice from one of the PCT guidebooks about encountering a cougar, that if I were to flee, I would surely die.

The more we walked, the less I worried about a few small rustles, knowing a squirrel would probably pop its head out from under a leaf. I also knew when I'd just avoided encountering a large animal such as a bear or an elk. Since I hiked alone more often than not, I sang out loud or used my hiking poles to hit rocks and other objects. I tried to make just enough noise for any animal I might be approaching to hear me first, and it worked quite a few times. I'd be singing and suddenly hear the ripping and snapping of bushes and tree branches just ahead of me as a large object thundered away from the trail. It was often out of my vision but always within ear shot. I would assume I had just disturbed a bear eating berries off the side of the trail that was too scared to wait and see how much of a threat I was.

Of all my senses and savvies that were heightened, I gained perhaps a completely new awareness that I never imagined could exist. Do you know at what point the moon is in its cycle right now? I certainly don't know without looking at my digital, satellite-connected, temperature-gauging clock that also tells me the moon cycle. But I knew the moon cycles on the trail. It wasn't that I felt the pull of the moon cycles, but that I literally saw the moon each night as I lay in our mesh-ceilinged tent, falling asleep to the moon's glow and subconsciously noting at what point it was in its cycle.

It was a strange knowledge of the surrounding environment to pick up on, but oddly satisfying in that I was so connected to the outside world that I could know at any given point what shape the moon would take on each evening. It wasn't an easy knowledge to maintain once we covered our upward-facing views with roofs after the trail was finished. I was sad when I realized I would no longer know the moon so well until I chose to live outside once again.

Because of all the strengthening in our senses, by the time we'd make it into town, it was a bit of sensory overload. Suddenly there were fluorescent lights with unforgiving harshness, TVs with high volumes and fast moving pictures, and cars with exhaust inhibiting our breathing. My ears often paid the price out of all my senses. They were accustomed to hearing a few voices at a time at the most, with subtle sounds of nature in the background. The day we hiked into Snoqualmie Pass in Central Washington, there were men clear-cutting parts of the forest that butted up against the trail. Upon hearing the tree chewing machines, I nearly jumped out of my skin because the sound was so piercingly loud. It was such a foreign sound to me that my first instinct was to find a hole to crawl into so I could protect myself from the noise. I can only imagine how frighteningly painful that sound must be to animals with a more heightened sense of hearing. I doubt animals enjoy living in our human environment with all the jarring sensory experiences that we've invented through machinery, modes of transportation, and entertainment.

There were also times when our senses failed us, or when we just weren't tuned into them. Early on in Southern California, we ran across a rattlesnake coiled up inches from the side of the trail. I was walking briskly downhill and had brushed the side of the snake with my pant leg, waking it up and angering it for the next hiker. Unfortunately that next hiker was Optimist. I heard the rustle of the snake hissing and coiling up, getting ready to strike, and had assumed it was just another lizard scurrying up the loose rock. About three seconds later I heard Optimist yell, "Oh shit!" and turned to see him dig his heels into the ground to stop himself and quickly back up. The snake's head was cocked back and ready to strike Optimist if he came any closer. It was so well camouflaged that when Optimist took his eyes off the snake to get his camera, he couldn't find the snake again to take its picture. It hadn't even moved an inch. If it had moved we would have been in trouble; we had such problems seeing it as it sat still, and we were just a few feet away from it. Our sense of sight failed us as we lost the snake among the loose brown rocks of the trail, and our sense of hearing learned a new sound: the eerie, hair-raising sound of a rattlesnake as it coiled and readied to strike.

The strange part about the enhancement of our senses, especially our sense of smell, is that it didn't apply to our own body odor. I know I must have been emitting some extremely ripe, pungent fumes, but I couldn't smell a thing. The only time I knew I smelled was when we were cramped in a car. Even with the windows down, I knew I stunk. Years after finishing the trail, I can still get a whiff of myself through my old hiking gear, which is tucked carefully away in an outdoor closet.

Perhaps my sense of smell didn't apply to my own body because there were a lot of parts of the trail that I found to be glorified. One of those parts was bathing. The image of bathing in crystal clear lakes, with the sun shining and a warm rock on which to dry was just that: an image. It was hardly the reality of my experience. There *was* an abundance of creeks, lakes, and other sources of relatively clean water, but it was rare that I ever jumped in to clean off au natural. I didn't want to take the time out of our day to strip down, wash up, dry off and put on the same dirty clothes again.

More accurately, I really didn't mind being dirty. I came to embrace, and even love my dirtiness. With the exception of teeth brushing, at what other point in life is it ok to be so lax in personal hygiene as on a trail? My body was so covered in dirt most of the time that when I *did* shower, people said to me, "I thought you were a lot tanner! You're actually really white!"

The societal rules of cleanliness just didn't apply along the trail, and our sense of dirty and clean became quite different the longer we called the outdoors our home.

In addition to bathing, using the outdoors as my latrine was much less scary than I originally expected it to be. This part of living outside that I dreaded and thought that I'd absolutely hate was actually one of the easiest parts of hiking. Peeing and pooping outside just wasn't that big of a deal. It wasn't as if I could hold it between towns so I always had a flushing toilet to accompany my bathroom breaks. I was forced to adjust my mindset as to what an acceptable pit stop looked like, and after a while, I actually preferred the outdoors to an enclosed throne.

I've learned a lot from the trail, many things being quite practical. I know that if I REALLY have to go to the bathroom, all I need to do is find some bushes to hide behind and dig a little hole if need be. Our first night after finishing the trail, we spent the night outside the Greyhound bus station in Vancouver, BC. We were visited by quite a few interesting people over the course of the night. One was a drunken woman who really needed to pee. She wouldn't stop talking about how badly she had to pee, and that none of the bathrooms were open at three in the morning. After a while I wanted to say, "Look, just go over behind that bench, squat down among the bushes, and shut up about it!"

It's amazing how the things that seem so foreign and uncomfortable at first become second nature when it's a lifestyle for months.

Sometimes I find myself staring out the window at work or at home. I can see the sun shining and the breeze blowing. Just imagining what they feel like allows me to put myself outside, standing on the trail, looking out into miles of mountains. I can feel the wind teasing my ponytail and whipping untamed strands of hair across my face, getting caught in the corners of my mouth and eyes. I can feel myself as both a separate entity from the outside world and as an important participant. I feel like I belong out there, among the mountains, among the trees, among the plants, and even among the animals, finding a way to live my life freely yet within a set of unspoken rules.

Looking back on the trail, one thing I remember the most is the blue sky. It's a deep, crisp blue that can't be seen on even the clearest days in an urban setting. Only on the trail can you look out and fully take in the vast, far-reaching blue sky. It's a visual that often gets stuck in my head, seeing myself perched atop the side of a mountain, looking out at the landscape before me, my view completely filled with blue skies and rolling mountains. It's a view that only partially comes through in pictures, that can only be understood in a first-hand experience. I'd like to think that I appreciated every blue sky that was there to greet me in the morning as I woke up and started walking.

I had many days where I was overwhelmed by my surroundings. I was amazed that such a naturally beautiful environment could exist at the same time as our human, often bland, concrete environment exists. It was early on the hike when we reached the highest point in Southern California near Mt. Baden-Powell. The lookout offered panoramic views of mountains and sky. It was a sight that few would believe exists amidst the bustle of Southern California and the far-reaching tentacles of the land of Los Angeles. It was a view that I could have spent hours looking at, like waves of the ocean or the flames of a campfire. It drew me in and though it made me feel tiny in the scale of time and land mass, it still made me feel special for being allowed to be in its presence.

By the time we made it to Washington, I was jaded from the beauty of the natural world surrounding us, yet at the same time I was still trying to be grateful for its presence. We had hiked over two thousand miles and were quickly closing in on the hundred-day mark of living outside. We had seen a lot of natural beauty.

If there were a statement I would take back if I could, it would be when I told a stranger, "I've seen enough pretty views."

It was in response to her suggestion that we walk a bit further up the trail for our snack break so that we could eat in the presence of a breathtaking scene in central Washington. For her it was the most beautiful view she'd seen in her entire week's worth of hiking, maybe even in her entire life. She was so proud to share it with a thru-hiker, yet I crushed her enthusiasm by plopping down on a simple rock off the side of the trail with my bag of granola in my lap, too grinch-like to even give her so much as a smile. It is a moment which I'm not proud of, and it's my own personal reminder that I will never reach full saturation from all the natural beauty surrounding me, nor should I ever take that readily available beauty for granted.

It took me a long time to fully appreciate the trail, and the first day was a testament to that fact. My mind was crowded with excitement, self-doubts and physical pain. All I could think to myself was, "Why in the world did I sign up for this?" and "How soon will this be over?" In those first few hours of walking, all I could think about were how many miles I had to cover in order to get to Canada.

As a cruel joke, there was actually a mile 1 marker on the trail, and when we hit that mile marker, someone had written in black marker below how many miles we had to go, which was over 2600. It almost made me cry. Me, being new to long-distance hiking, blurted out, "I wish we were already at the end with just one mile to go!" Three pairs of feet stopped in their tracks and three shocked faces turned to look at me, with Animal questioning me, "Are you crazy? I don't want this to be over yet!"

At that point, I certainly did.

For Optimist, Rocketcop and Animal, the trail wasn't about getting from Mexico to Canada. It was about the experiences in between. Getting to Canada was just another part of the long-distance hike. It took a long time for that idea to sink in for me, as I just couldn't wrap my mind around hiking from point A to point B without having the goal of getting to point B. The only thing that mattered to them was the line between A and B, and how rich in experiences that line was. The bolder the line, the better. The more they recognized that it was the line that mattered at the present moment, the more deeply they lived in that moment over any future finishing point. I didn't fully appreciate the idea of enjoying the experience until I got to Manning Park, Canada and cried on Optimist's shoulder because we had reached the end and had no miles left to walk.

The PCT may end on the border of the US and Canada, but another trail continues for about eight more miles before it reaches the first road to actually get off the trail. It was a good thing someone prepared me for those extra eight miles early on. I just may have had a temper tantrum right there at the end, angry that there wasn't a bus full of balloons, pizza and ice cream waiting to greet me, feed me, and take my picture. Those extra eight miles were the only way off the trail.

Though I dreaded them the entire hike, as if eight miles were going to break me after walking over 2600, they were bittersweet miles full of victory and sadness.

Our grand adventure had ended at the border, and those eight miles were our chance to acclimate ourselves to society again. Though we had changed over the course of our journey, everyone else around us had kept spinning in their own small worlds without us. I took those last eight miles as an opportunity to look around me and take it all in. I knew I'd never be in that same sort of physical and mental state again, no matter how hard I might try. I mentally photographed the entire walk so I could make sure I took something home just for myself, and I took in every last bite that my senses would ingest.

I realized in those last eight miles that though I may have cursed the trail's existence at times, I was still appreciative of every moment that the trail allowed me to be a temporary visitor in its home. It finally hit me that the opportunity for a life event such as thru-hiking a long distance trail may never cross my path again, and that I may have spent my life's allotted time with the outside world. Living that closely to nature for that long showed me that though we as humans might think of the world as tamed, it's as wild as ever. We can never truly take over the land, the forests, or the animals. If for some reason humans should no longer occupy the planet, nature will reclaim itself and go back to its natural state. It is just as you put your home back in order after a house guest's stay. You clean up after them, stripping the bed sheets, washing the towels, and putting the small, fragile items back in their places. After a while, it's as if they were never there.

Optimist and I took in as many experiences as our senses would allow, especially as our journey was coming to a close during the state of Washington. We ate all the berries that our stomachs would digest, I fully embraced dirt as part of my body, and we never stopped looking out into the endless expanse of mountains. The irony is that we were considered by some fellow hikers to be unappreciative of the trail simply because we hiked a lot of miles in one day, and because we moved up the trail relatively quickly. We were told that we weren't stopping to smell the roses. I don't recall seeing too many roses along the way, if any, but I certainly know I picked plenty of berries.

Optimist and I also didn't take many photographs of our experience. While we took a couple hundred photos, others took thousands. Somehow more photographs translated into a greater appreciation of the trail for many other hikers. There was nothing

Optimist and I could say to convince people otherwise, so we never let it bother us. We didn't have to convince ourselves that at times we were in complete awe of our surroundings. We didn't measure our level of gratefulness towards nature's beauty by the amount of pictures taken, the number of days outside, or the amount of breaks taken. My memories and the mental journeys my senses allow me to take are proof enough for me.

None of us will ever truly appreciate our environment until it's gone, in which case we might not be around either. Until then, I know I did my best in breathing in the entire trail through all my senses and holding those experiences in my mind for later remembrance and reverence.

8 PRACTICE HUMILITY

This lesson could just as easily be titled, "Don't step up on that pedestal if you're not willing to step down again."

That might be a bit long for the purposes of summing up a lesson in a few words, but it best describes the constant ups and downs that I experienced along the trail. My ego would swell at some moments, lifting me off the ground and into the clouds. It would then deflate at other moments, sending me into a spiral of self-doubt, self-pity, and self-realization. While it's healthy to be humbled, it's not exactly fun, and though we should all welcome a humbling experience for its eye-opening reality checks, we shun it like an incoming call from our least favorite relative.

Humility calls us often, and on those rare occasions that we take a deep breath and just answer the call, we realize that it's not so bad after all. We discover that it's relatively quick and painless, and that there might actually be something to gain from having answered the phone. We often feel better once we've hung up and simply gutted out the call, and sometimes, we even enjoy it.

Humility was hard to avoid on the trail. There was only so much I could do to put it off, to let it go to voicemail. There was nowhere to hide. It was a raw lifestyle without any distractions, and without any ways to fake it. The miles were up to me to walk. I was often left with only my mind to talk to, and I had to think of a lot to say to myself.

My mind ran through the gamut of thoughts along the trail, and every emotion rolled through me and often off my cheeks in the form of tears. I had to face emotions I never thought possible, situations that would break most people both mentally and physically, and still, all I was doing was walking. It's hard to believe that walking outside would elicit anything other than the basic needs of thirst, hunger and sleep. Yet, the trail was much more than basic. It was not as black and white as some would have you believe, that all you need to do is to keep moving one foot in front of the other. The mind has to decide to allow those feet to move in the first place.

I had a hard time keeping my mind out of the decision process to keep my feet moving, and an equally hard time striking the balance between keeping my ego in check and keeping the trail from crushing me. There are all kinds of obstacles in the way of a thru-hiker, one of the biggest being the ego. It's easy to get full of oneself after finishing a ten day string of hiking thirty miles a day. It's also just as easy to lose it all mentally and physically for that matter, with one small slip during a dangerous river crossing or a mountain pass covered in snow.

The pedestal is always there for a hiker. It's easy to climb aboard it, but once atop it, it's also just as easy to get scared of heights, the fall seemingly much worse than that from the view on the ground. I was constantly avoiding the pedestal yet wanting the fake sense of confidence that it brought. In the end I realized I could have the confidence without the pedestal and that I would be humbled by the trail no matter what height I fell from.

The best way I've ever heard someone describe the swing in emotions and even status while being on an adventure such as thru-hiking the PCT was by one of our good friends, Matt (not to be confused with Optimist Matt). He describes it as the ability to feel like both a celebrity and a refugee, all in the same day.

With adventures like the PCT, the stakes are high for both success and failure. You are putting yourself out there with high risks, and the results could swing heavily in your favor or crushingly against you. You are a stranger among the wild, trying to fit into a lifestyle so far removed from your own, trying to hurdle mental and physical obstacles, and hopefully trying to enjoy it all at the same time. It's not easy, so when something goes right, you are giddy with happiness and pride. When something goes wrong, there are few shoulders to cry on, and even fewer comforts to crawl into. If you are having a bad day, there are not beds to curl up in, or movies to watch while lying on the couch. There is no pause button on the trail life, and the luxuries of an indoor lifestyle couldn't be any further from your current state.

While hiking the PCT, I felt the swing in status often from a celebrity to a refugee. If we were in towns, people that knew about the PCT would lather us in praise for attempting the thru-hike. Many of them offered up their own water, food, and even maps, just because we were out there hiking.

Several even took our pictures with them, and often asked us for advice. Twice we had strangers ask if they could camp with us for the evening or hike with us for a few hours, just so they could hear our stories and be around us. Some campers actually admitted to us that they sought out thru-hikers and hoped to meet some. It was as if we were a rare species that few got the chance to see in real-life action. I've never felt so much admiration, nor have I ever been so inspired by the willingness in others to help us.

Even if people didn't know about the PCT, the awe and amazement in their voices was alone enough to blow air into our heads. Our favorite questions to answer from these types of people were, "Where are you coming from?" and, "How long have you been out here?" How cool would you feel if you were in the middle of Oregon and able to answer, "Mexico," knowing your own feet carried you there? Or if you were able to say, "I've been living outside for ninety-seven days, and I'm still going"? Just the reactions from the people questioning you would probably stir up some pride in your head, no matter how hard you'd try to squelch it. To this day I can't help but feel that stir when someone who only knows me on the surface finds out that I walked from Mexico to Canada. The inundation of wide-eyed questions is impossible to avoid and equally fun to entertain.

Overall, people treated us like we were doing the coolest thing in the world by hiking the PCT. I even had a little girl of twelve years tell me she wanted to be just like me when she grew up, a woman thru-hiking the PCT. I was so flattered that I was speechless, unable to recover from the sincerity and belief in her tiny, yet powerful voice. I wasn't sure I even believed in myself that strongly.

By the time we made it past Central California and were well into Northern California, past the halfway point, the atmosphere on the trail felt different. It felt much less crowded. We didn't see as many people on a daily basis, the number of trail journals along the way dwindled, and the main pack seemed to have scattered. I quickly learned from the trail grapevine that this wasn't just a feeling. It was in fact reality. Many people had pulled off the trail by Tuolumne Meadows (around mile

940) or shortly thereafter. To learn this fact, that I'd already made it much further than many others attempting the thru-hike, boosted my confidence even more. Not only did I have the praise from others building me up, but now I was patting myself on the back. This coupling of pride could only lead me astray from humility.

Imagine how I felt by the time I made it to Washington. The trail became downright deserted of other thru-hikers compared to the seemingly endless stream in Southern California. I felt like a miles machine that could handle anything thrown my way, especially since others didn't seem capable as they were no longer on the trail. My pride in my feats thus far had led me so far as to feel worthy of being a guest on a talk show, as if others should look at my accomplishments and be in awe. One of my favorite games that I played to pass the time and to make myself feel better was to mentally interview myself. I would pretend I was sitting in a comfortable armchair next to Oprah or Ellen, the spotlight on me as I answered the same questions that poured from so many people that met us. "What did you eat…How heavy was your pack…Where did you sleep…Were you scared of bears…?"

I knew it was silly and so far from reality, but at that point I wanted more praise for what I was doing. The praise from other trail people was not enough to legitimize my hike. I wanted it to be known on a much greater level what an accomplishment I was achieving. Accomplishing the thru-hike meant that I was going so far out of my scope of abilities and actually succeeding, that humility was not so easy for me to remember. I was in severe danger of not practicing humility and in danger of completely losing sight of myself within the big picture the more I actually succeeded in the thru-hike.

Fortunately, pride never lasted very long. The moment I would start to get a big head, thinking of myself as invincible, I usually tripped on a rock, quickly reminded that I was just a speck of life in the grand scheme of the trail. I can't count the number of times my bumbling feet tripped over tree roots, slipped on rocks in creek crossings, or outright failed me and caused me to stumble forward out of control and land on my hands or face. I could have easily been named Ms. Graceful with the number of mishaps my feet got me into.

Reality would also hit me hard when we left towns. Basking in the praise of others would be great until I remembered that I still had to put in a lot of miles to actually *become* a thru-hiker.

Each time we left a town, mid-sections protruding from pizza and pride swelling from townspeople's praise, I would mentally step down from my throne and start walking again. I still had to face the miles, the thirst, the food cravings, the dirty, smelly clothes, and the tent as my shelter each day. It was always a humbling experience to face the trail after any sort of absence, even after something as simple as a five minute snack break.

What lingered with me most about encounters with others along the trail was the overwhelming feeling of admiration that was pouring from them. It was unconditional, as if we could do no wrong, and as if we represented everything good and holy about long-distance hiking and about the PCT.

With less than two weeks to go in the hike, I realized why that bothered me.

I knew it was wrong to take all the credit and admiration from others, because it wasn't me that was so great. It was the trail. The trail held the beauty, the experiences, and the challenges. I was simply renting time and space, hoping to earn an inkling of the joy that came in walking the entire thing. I was just a temporary resident in a tiny span of time on a piece of life that could crush me with its wildness at any moment. The trail in fact owned me and could only break me. There was never any possibility that I would humble the trail. Only finishing it could make the trail feel a little less powerful.

With each new mountain pass that we crossed and each new park that we entered, the strength and power in nature asserted itself in enormous, intimidating beauty. Just the views alone were humbling. To look out and only see signs of Mother Nature surrounding me was a bit frightening at times, yet inspiring that such a place still exists in the concrete world that surrounds most of us.

I learned to step back from the pedestal that others and even I would cast in front of me. I was hesitant to step up for fear of losing myself in pride, and of taking advantage of others' staunch belief in the greatness of our actions. I literally said to myself, "Stay humble and attribute praise to the trail itself. You are only a human, and this trail will be here well after you are not. Do not confuse your own greatness with that of the trail."

While others and I were always there to build me up to celebrity status, those same people, along with the trail itself, were always there to tear me down to a refugee. The same clothes were on my back as the day before, I was always hungry, and a tent was my home. Each and every day the trail was there to put me in my place.

One piece of the trail that I cannot do any justice in describing is just how hard it was. It is not easy to walk from Mexico to Canada with your life of your back. Try walking for one day with a forty-pound pack on your back for twenty five miles. It is not easy to be hungry or thirsty all the time, visions of food and drink constantly clouding your vision as you walk. I shudder as I remember how crazy my cravings for chips and ice cream made me as we neared towns. It is not easy to be so dirty for days on end that even you would not want to be in an enclosed space with yourself. It is not easy to call a tent your shelter each night, let alone to sleep on a thin piece of foam as your mattress. I can almost feel the bruises on my hips from sleeping on my side on the hard ground. I just never had trouble sleeping on sore hips on the ground because I was too darn tired to notice or care. I still have scars on my hips from the blisters caused by a heavy pack, and for a long time I could still see the area on my lower back where my heavy pack grinded into the salt build-up on my shorts and created a bright red, bleeding rash.

And those are only the difficult puzzle pieces of living outside for days on end. That doesn't even include how difficult the trail actually was. Southern California's challenges were the coupling of a lack of water and heat that was all encompassing, with little shade to lower the temperature. Central California brought forth such steep, long climbs and descents that depleted every ounce of energy in me. I was in tears at times because I just didn't want to keep going. Though I prayed for flat ground, all I got were hills and mountains, which only went up or down. Northern California and Oregon had a combination of several factors, such as heat, massive climbs and descents in and out of towns, fewer hikers on the trail for support, and mileage burnout from having hiked so many miles, yet still having so many to go. Washington was marked by its volatility in weather. It could be sunny and seventy degrees at one moment, then a front would move in and drop the temperature by twenty degrees and bring with it pouring rain for three days straight. Try being wet for three days in fifty degree temperatures. It is miserable. Again, there is no pause button, no escape button to magically pull off the trail into a warm, dry home and make it all better. Believe me, I searched it out like a kid at an Easter egg hunt, but always came up short.

I will never be able to describe how hard it is to thru-hike a long distance trail such as the PCT. You cannot truly know until you try it. It's always ironic when I talk to others about the trail. While I have stars in my eyes talking about how great of an experience it was, I know in the back of my mind that it brought me to tears. I know that at times, I cursed its existence and myself for beginning such a challenge. I know I had mental breakdowns that caused me to stop walking and question everything, and I know it physically sapped me of all strength. At times, it seemed like all the trail was trying to do was humble me, even if I didn't feel I needed it. Sometimes I felt like screaming, "You can stop beating me up now, trail! I get it. You're bigger than me, tougher than me, and I'll never truly conquer you, so just let up a little!"

While the trail itself was difficult, I had legendary moments of self-inflicted humility, where the trail had nothing to do with beating me down into normal human status. My own stupidity filled in for the trail. These kind of experiences reminded me of how human and how vulnerable I was, and just how much I needed to take a step back and be honest with myself rather than hold myself in any sort of high regard.

There was one particular experience that I will never forget, nor will I ever live down. It was a moment when I felt especially humbled, when I really did have to laugh at myself and forget any kind of pride that I'd accumulated thus far.

On the second day in the Central California section, we ate lunch at the Chicken Spring Lake, around mile 750. We had just left Kennedy Meadows the day before, so we had packs full of food from our resupply at the town's general store. When packs were full of food, it was always tempting to eat a little more not only because it was there, but also because it meant lessening the pack weight faster.

After eating lunch, I snacked on a few pieces of dried fruit for dessert. A few pieces of snacking became inhaling the entire one pound bag. It was a very bad decision. My excuse was that it didn't feel like my mind had made the choice to eat the whole bag. My hands and mouth seemed separate from my brain, mindlessly popping piece after piece into my anxiously chewing mouth.

In normal life, I would have been appalled at eating an entire bag of anything. Since calorie counting occupied less than a sliver of my thoughts while hiking, I quickly got over the fact that I ate hundreds of calories for my dessert. I was only disappointed in myself in not making the dried fruit last at least a few days' worth of snacking. Other than that blip of a thought, I continued hiking with Optimist up the trail.

About a half hour later, just after entering the Sequoia National Park border, I went to fart. It was something that I did quite often in the open air, a part of the trail that I truly miss. There are very few lifestyles where farting freely without consequences is one of the perks.

My insides had been bubbling and popping ever since lunch. I could feel a lot of movement going on with all the digesting of my recent lunch. My fart stopped me in my tracks as my seemingly harmless pocket of air turned into much more than a fart or even a shart. I had completely pooped my pants. The whole pound of dried fruit had already worked its way through me, or had forced everything else out ahead of it to make room for its poundage.

I stood there frozen as soon as I felt it leave my body. Optimist was just ahead of me, and I whispered to him, "Optimist, I think I just pooped my pants."

I didn't dare move an inch.

He turned around to face me, stunned but also poised to start laughing, a smile forming.

Standing there watching Optimist in a gaze of half awe/half amusement wasn't a great option. I could see he wasn't going to do much to help me. I quickly, yet cautiously, made my way about fifteen feet off the trail and ducked behind a tree in order to inspect the damage. Optimist was still watching me, grinning widely as I proceeded to take off my shorts right there in the open. The tree wasn't that big in diameter for any sort of privacy, but that was the least of my problems.

It was bad. I mean, *really* bad. I had not only pooped my pants, but I also pooped a semi-liquid mess. It filled my shorts, covered my butt, and was quickly making its way down my thighs. I could not understand how so much came out in one harmless, seemingly effortless push of a fart.

All I could do was damage-control at that point. I begged Optimist to bring me the roll of toilet paper so I could clean myself first. Once that was done, I put on my town shorts, a clean pair of black running shorts that were reserved strictly for sleeping or town time. I hated the thought of hiking in them and possibly pooping in them too, but I had no choice. It was either hike naked, in my one pair of underwear, which

I did seriously consider as I stood there half-naked, or in my clean running shorts. I chose the running shorts.

I wiped as much poop off my hiking shorts as I could. Then I balled the pants up and put them in a spare plastic bag, hoping I could wash them at an upcoming water source. Later that evening we camped near a creek that became my washing machine and allowed me to once again wear the semi-clean, poopy hiking pants.

Pooping my pants was my own undoing, as were all the times that I tripped or fell, but they were all checkmarks on the list of humbling experiences along the way. It's an experience that I will never live down, but that I can now laugh about in remembering.

With each slip, with each fall, with each accidental pants pooping, which thankfully only numbered one, I learned more and more that if I was going to fully embrace the trail and its relationship to me, to being a human that errs, I was going to have to practice humility. The realization hit me much harder when a slip or fall would follow a moment of basking in lavish praise or a moment where I hadn't yet stepped down from my mental pedestal.

There were times on the trail when I didn't receive the admiration from others that I expected would pour from them so easily, and it really threw me for a loop. Because so many people were quick to praise us, I took it for granted after a while.

Near Lake Tahoe in Central California, Optimist and I stopped at Echo Lake's general store, closing in on eleven hundred miles. It was a warm day and I spent my time that afternoon sitting outside the store, eating a waffle cone of ice cream. Optimist talked on our cell phone and paced around the picnic benches just in front of the building. I was perfectly content sitting there on the storefront's stone wall, enjoying the heat of the late afternoon's sun and the coolness of my cookies n' cream cone.

As I sat there, a group of four older women walked up to the store. They were just finishing a day hike. Each of them carried a small backpack, they wiped beads of sweat from their foreheads as they approached the store, and two of them carried hiking poles. All of them had silver hair and moved their bodies with an old age caution that my muscles and bones had not yet learned. As each of them saw my ice cream, their eyes lit up at the prospect of ice cream, and they made their way inside for a treat of their own. Eventually they came back outside, one by one, with ice cream or some other sweet vice.

They all took a seat around me on the stone wall, lifting their faces to the sun with their eyes closed and their lips turned up in a smile.

They asked me a little bit about thru-hiking the trail, and I asked them about their hiking as well, but it wasn't the same conversation I seemed to have with so many strangers. They didn't exude admiration or awe at my feat. They didn't pour twenty questions on me about the trail life. Heck, I think they expected me to ask them more questions about their hiking because it was such an oddity to see four older women out there on the rugged trail. They didn't even stay seated next to me for very long. As soon as each cone was finished, or the last sip of water was taken, they stood up, ready to move on. Normally I was the first one to leave, the questions still flowing from others as I packed up my things and headed up the trail.

As I watched them cross the parking lot together, it occurred to me that I must have seemed commonplace to them. I was just another young buck out there able to handle a heavy pack and a lot of miles. What was I doing that was really special? How was my trail experience much different from those around me? What was I really making of myself and of my time on the trail? All these thoughts went through my head as I sat there watching these women carry themselves.

Long after they left me, I finally realized that *they* were the interesting ones. Though they may have all been someone's grandmothers, they were tough women that weren't about to let age determine what activities their bodies and minds could do. They were fighting all age stereotypes, and winning handedly. As I sat on the stone wall, stunned in the wake of their self-confidence and in their lack of interest in me, I realized I had expected praise for which I wasn't worthy.

Suddenly I wasn't so cool. All I was doing was walking a really long way, doing it amidst self-inflicted, chosen pain, and leaving a cloud of dirt and stench in my wake. I felt very small and unimportant in the grand scheme of life. My expectations of others' praise certainly changed after that day.

I did cheat on the last day of the hike, day one hundred and nine, and allowed for the accumulation of pride. It was of course a bad idea. We were on the mental throne all day, knowing that we'd reached the end and accomplished our PCT thru-hike. We met six people on the trail that day, all of them equally happy as us to hear we had made it the entire way. They seemed to understand what it meant to walk from

Mexico to Canada. They knew we were on our last miles of an incredible journey, and it was praise and admiration that I was glad to accept. I was feeling pretty darn good about myself at that point. We were celebrities again.

The day was beautiful with sun and blue skies, and the trail miles were easy because they were the last of them. I savored the time with Optimist. Before I knew it, we popped out of the trail and onto a road where we saw cars, people and buildings. Optimist turned to me and said, "Well, that's it. We're finished."

It was an overwhelming feeling to be finished. For the last three and a half months, I tried to *not* think about what it would feel like to be done, for fear of teasing myself. Yet there we were, completely finished with zero miles left to walk. I broke down in tears and Optimist wrapped his arms around me. My tears streaked the dirt around my eyes and my cheeks. I would have never thought my reaction would be tears upon finishing. I think the fear was beginning to set in. The fear of the unknown world after the end of a thru-hike, and the fear of not having my day so predictably laid out for me anymore. Optimist and I had no plans for what was next in life. It was scary and exciting at the same time.

Once we recovered from the shock of being finished, we thought about what was next on the agenda, which was to figure out a way to food, shelter, and possibly a shower. We knew all of those things were at the Manning Park campground. As we stood there on the side of the road, we saw a parking lot with a few cars and several people milling around the signs at the trailhead. They didn't look like hikers. They wore clean dress clothes, their shoes were far from anything athletic, and the women were wearing enough makeup that it was doubtful they were expecting to exert energy to the point of sweating.

We asked them for directions to Manning Park, as the signs were in discrepancy with our book. The road pointed in one direction and our book said to go the other way, so we assumed they'd know which way to go. As we asked for directions, all of them looked at us cautiously, showing no recognition or knowledge that they were standing at the end of a 2600 mile trail. It was as if they'd never seen hikers before. They pointed us in the right direction down the road and turned away from us, not interested in continuing the conversation. As we walked up the road and neared the entrance towards the park, we saw one of the women who had just spoken to us drive right past us and enter into the park. She had known she was going exactly where we wanted to go, yet had not offered us a ride. She even waved at us as she drove by. We felt miffed and even hurt by the lack of trail magic the moment we stepped off the trail. Why hadn't she helped us? So far along the trail, all others would have opened their car doors and practically loaded our gear for us in their trunks. We certainly weren't in Kansas anymore. Trail magic did not go beyond the boundaries of the trail.

Once we made it to the park, we finished early enough in the day to catch a bus to Vancouver, BC. It was our next stopping point along the route back to the U.S. Unfortunately, we were scheduled to arrive in Vancouver at 9:30 p.m., on Canada's (and the US's) Labor Day weekend. Every local hostel and hotel was likely to be booked. We found this out from a woman on the bus who warned us that it would be difficult to find a place to sleep in Vancouver. We thought she might be our hope of a trail angel off the trail, but her help ended at the extent of that warning.

She was right. Once we arrived in Vancouver and walked the area around the bus station in search of a place to stay, we found there was no room at any inn in Vancouver.

We walked back to the bus station with our heads hanging low at our prospects for shelter for the evening. The first bus to Seattle wasn't until the next morning, and on top of that, the bus station closed its doors from 1:00 a.m. to 5:00 a.m. We couldn't just stay in there all night. As a last ditch effort, I pleaded with the night shift employee to let us pitch our tent inside since we'd just finished the PCT. Since he had no idea what that was or why it should make us important, it was a lost cause. He had to follow the rules and make us leave, and we certainly weren't worth breaking them. The night guard at the bus station did assure us that it was perfectly legal to sleep on the sidewalk of the bus station, and that there were security cameras in case anything should happen.

"Great, *now* we feel safe!" we said to ourselves as we wondered how often things in fact happened to warrant the use of the cameras.

Rather than the welcoming party of balloons, pizza, and ice cream that I'd dreamed would meet us at the finish, we slept outside the Greyhound bus station on the day we completed our walk from Mexico to Canada. We suddenly relinquished our status of star thru-hikers to homeless, dirty bums. Every part of our look and situation screamed homeless to all that walked by the bus station. We were refugees once again.

It was the ultimate reality check. It was such a quick change in emotion from being held in such high regard on the trail earlier that day, to later being looked at like we were useless members of society because we were dirty, smelly and sleeping on the sidewalk in sleeping bags. There was no discernable difference between us and the homeless. I wanted to stick a sign above my head, telling people what I'd just accomplished, that I wasn't homeless, that I had a set of bad circumstances getting into town so late, and that I actually had money in my bank account. Instead, I swallowed my pride and tried to ignore the *real* homeless people sleeping outside the bus station. My previously blurred visions of their hardships were suddenly much clearer now that I was considered to be included in their circle.

The only thing that kept me afloat that night was knowing that I had a bus ticket to Seattle the next day, along with a plane ticket home to Ohio after that. I knew my pizza and ice cream would simply have to wait. As Matt said, life often swings you from a celebrity to a refugee, all in the same day. The only way I could find to deal with that shift was to practice humility.

The most difficult part about practicing humility is also taking in the realization that we cannot control everything. There are going to be times when no matter what we do, we cannot swing the outcome of a situation. All we can do is swing our reaction to that outcome. We cannot stop the rain from coming down on us, nor can we keep our tent from getting soaked under constant downpour. But, we can adjust our attitude in those difficult times and do our best to keep our minds positive and keep all our other gear dry.

On one hand, a lack of control is frustrating. I often felt like a shirt in a washing machine, being pulled around and tugged at, not able to choose my next move. On the other hand, it's freeing to know that not everything is up to us. Part of the experience is knowing that we will not expect everything that will be thrown our way, but that we'll have to figure it out as we go. I doubt many people start a long-distance trail with the thought, "Ok, I've planned everything out for the next several months. I know exactly what's going to happen. Now let's put that plan into action without any speed bumps or detours."

Sometimes the detours are the best part, because they take us to a place, physically and even mentally, that we may have never gone to otherwise. Oftentimes, we are better for having taken that route.

For me it was always humbling to look out into the distance, into the mountains, knowing that they were capable of throwing obstacles my way that no amount of planning would prepare me for. I would simply have to go with the flow, ride it out, and see where I came out on the other side.

There are so many factors ready and waiting to humble us, including the trail, other people, and even ourselves, that to swell with pride will only lead us to a false sense of confidence. It will only make the fall that much further from the ground or that much harder when we hit it.

To this day I take pride in accomplishing the thru-hike, a feat that few can claim. But, with that pride comes the humbling memories of just how hard the entire experience was day in and day out. It was not all fun and games the entire way, and I'd be ashamed if I gave that impression to those who don't know what the experience is like. I have too much respect for the trail to pretend that my achievement is anything beyond just that. I achieved what I set out to do, to walk from Mexico to Canada along the PCT. I was just lucky that my own ego didn't get too much in the way of allowing me to do so.

Practicing humility is accepting the lows with the highs, knowing the highs are that much better for having experienced the lows. It's accepting that we're human but still reaching for seemingly impossible goals. It is knowing that pedestals are merely a temptation to stop when all we should do is just keep walking.

9 HIKE YOUR OWN HIKE

We did the entire trail all wrong. At least that's what people told us.

From day one all the way to the finish, every major part of our trail experience caused controversy between us and other thru-hikers and even several trail angels. To many people, we did the trail all wrong. But for Optimist and me, the methods by which we made it from Mexico to Canada, on every step of the Pacific Crest National Scenic Trail, were done our way.

It was perfect. Perfectly ours.

Planning for an adventure such as the PCT is like putting together a puzzle. Everyone has common types of pieces like the four corners, the edges and the middle. Only, every individual's puzzle is different in what those pieces look like and how they fit together. How each of those pieces looks and how a person puts that puzzle together can vary widely.

All trail puzzles involve some means of walking, carrying belongings, and eating and resting, at the very least. Past those must-have elements of a thru-hike, it's up to the individual to decide just how much they want to walk each day, how much or how little stuff they'd like to carry, how much food to both carry and eat each day, and just how many breaks they'd like along the way.

What's even more unique about these pieces is that they are constantly changing and morphing as a hiker moves north. Just because a person sets out to average twenty miles a day, or to stop for food every three to five days, doesn't mean they are stuck to that plan the entire way. There is no pigeonholing in the puzzle making. There is plenty of time to move pieces around in order to make a better fit, and there is no allegiance to one certain way of thru-hiking because there is more than one way to hike a trail.

While there is not one way to hike a trail, there are norms. Just like there are norms in society of how people live, in terms of going to school, getting a job, having a family…there are norms on the trail. Many people mold their trail puzzle based on what people have done in the past and what people around them are doing. It's an easier way to tackle the challenge of hiking the trail because it takes some of the thinking out of the equation, knowing certain ways have worked for others.

Examining the norms as part of the planning for the trail is a great way to set up the puzzle. It becomes a negative way to build a puzzle when a person doesn't let themselves or others stray from the norms in order to piece together their own personal trail puzzle. When the choice is taken out of how to thru-hike, controversy is inevitable.

A major piece of the PCT puzzle is when a person actually starts the thru-hike. The seasons deem when a thru-hike is possible, as the Southern California section increases in heat and a lack of water the further the calendar is past late April. But, one cannot start too early, as the snow needs time to melt in the Sierra Nevada in Central California. Later up the trail, finishing times must be planned around the possibility of snow in Northern Washington beginning as early as September. Due to the combination of all these factors, most hikers begin at the Mexico border in mid-April.

There is even an official kick-off party each year. Past thru-hikers and trail lovers gather around a campground about twenty miles into the trail to greet the year's crop of thru-hikers and to send them off into the lion's mouth, or so it feels. Most hikers start around the kick-off party, with a few stragglers starting earlier because they are possibly slower hikers, or some starting later due to choice or circumstance.

As we were planning for the hike, we knew the earliest day we would be able to start was May 16. Optimist finished graduate school on May 12 in Annapolis, Maryland. We gave ourselves three days between graduation and day one of the hike to move our things to his parents' home in Ohio, give our goodbyes to family and friends, and fly out to San Diego.

Before we had even started the trail, many people who knew about thru-hiking the PCT were quick to offer their opinion as to why we were getting off on the wrong foot. We were told that our planned start date of May 16 was too late, that we would be around no other hikers, that it would be too dry and hot in Southern California, and that we wouldn't have enough time to make it to Canada before the first snowfall. The list of late start consequences kept going. I admit, I was a bit skeptical myself as to how we were going to surmount all the threatening effects that came with beginning our hike so late in the season compared to the main pack of thru-hikers.

Despite the advice of others, we still started the trail on Wednesday, May 16, 2007. It was in fact a late start in comparison to the main pack of thru-hikers, but our options were limited given our circumstances. Putting aside all the dissenters, we simply knew we'd have to deal with the consequences as they came rather than force the hike to begin any earlier.

Another piece of the puzzle is the all-important resupply. Just to recap, a resupply is when a hiker stocks back up on food and other dwindling essentials at a nearby town, whether it be buying items at a grocery store, or mailing ahead boxes to post offices. Some people solely rely on groceries in towns along the way, and some people pack boxes ahead of time with someone at home mailing them. Most hikers do a combination of the two and most also plan this part of the trail with great detail before starting. They don't leave a whole lot to chance. It can be a very stressful, time-consuming part of the pre-trail planning to figure out how food is going to be obtained along the entire way.

There's a reason we were named Team Sherpa, and it's mainly because of our resupply strategy. Coming into the hike, we actually planned on not planning a resupply strategy. It simply made our heads spin to plan such a large piece of the puzzle ahead of time. We felt confident in ourselves to figure it out as we went. Also, our tastes changed so dramatically over the course of the hike, depending on the temperature, the difficulty of the terrain, and the elevation. We would have done ourselves a great injustice by sending ourselves a box of the exact same thing for the entire trail.

Early on in the hike, Optimist and I also decided that we didn't want to hitch-hike to towns off the trail. We wanted to walk to all of our resupply towns, unless we had a ride from family or friends. This was a big deal. Most towns were anywhere from five to twenty miles away from the trail. There was no such thing as a drive-thru along the trail, so only walking extra miles or hitching a ride led to food.

We decided this food strategy when we were hiking around Prozac, another thru-hiker, in the first week. She was quick to declare that it was impossible to resupply that way, pointing out that we'd have to go more than a mile off the trail in order to reach a town in Central California.

According to her, the mileage between towns was just too much. The stretch from Kennedy Meadows to Tuolumne Meadows was 237 miles. The lore of the trail was that hikers could only average fifteen miles a day through that section because it posed such difficult climbs and descents. Do the math and that's nearly sixteen days of food to carry. Do the math again, and it's at least thirty pounds of just food, in addition to any other pack weight. Prozac had a good point.

From then on, because she said it couldn't be done, it became our challenge to resupply in towns within a mile of the trail. We adopted this method and carried it out the entire way, with the few exceptions where family or friends picked us up off the trail for towns further away.

This strategy confirmed that we were in fact different from the norm. Most other hikers hitched rides from strangers or actually walked the extra miles to solve this dilemma. Hitching was relatively safe considering most people driving those roads knew about the PCT. We simply chose to not rely on hitching as a mode of transportation and we hated extra miles. Thus, Team Sherpa was born and we agreed to only resupply in towns within a mile of the trail.

The name Team Sherpa stuck. We inevitably had long stretches of food carries and heavy packs. We also had to make sure we covered enough miles during the day to shorten the time between towns as much as possible. We covered the 237 mile stretch from Kennedy Meadows to Tuolumne in ten days, averaging almost twenty four miles a day, nine more a day than what was thought possible. We hiked from sun up to sundown to make it, and we were ravenous by Tuolumne. There weren't too many towns within a mile of the trail, so the routine of heavy packs and high mileage became our norm. It definitely wasn't easy.

Our packs often weighed forty to fifty pounds on our way out of town, mainly because of food weight. Many towns were lower in elevation, so it was great cruising downhill into town with a near empty pack. On the flip side, it was that much more grueling to hike uphill out of town with a pack weighing heavily on our backs and legs.

We had a total of twelve resupplies over the course of the trail, averaging 220 miles between towns. In addition, we had six separate stops for treats that were immediately consumed and never touched our packs. This was the common fare of pizza and ice cream in places like Reds Meadows, California, and Hyatt Lake, Oregon. Those were the best kinds of resupplies. Our longest food carry was eleven days, 320 miles, from Crater Lake to Cascade Locks in Oregon. It covered most of the state of Oregon.

We even had a "Grand Finale" for the state of Washington. We only resupplied once at Snoqualmie Pass after 2400 miles, halfway through our twenty-day trek in the state. Achilles volunteered to join us in the Grand Finale challenge, but since he hadn't been "training" like we had with long resupplies, it didn't go over too well. In fact, he still hasn't truly forgiven us for dangling that challenge in front of him. We never actually intended for him to take us up on it.

For people who may not know much about long-distance hiking, this resupply strategy probably sounds just as normal as any other. There is no scale of relativity. We were far from the norm when it came to the resupply strategy of the majority of the pack. While the main pack was stopping every three to five days in towns, we were stopping every nine to eleven days. Anything over seven days of food seemed unimaginable to most others. This meant we carried anywhere from double to four times the amount of food as others. Equate that to pack weight, one of the all important factors of hiking. If someone was carrying five pounds of food, we were carrying twenty.

People were quick to bring up our differences, to question our methods. While we had perfectly legitimate reasoning as to why we carried such long food stretches, they often didn't want to hear it. They didn't want to admit that it could be done, or at least didn't want to hear just how true it was that there was more than one way to accomplish that part of a long-distance hike.

I remember standing in a general store aisle in Southern California, discussing the upcoming stretch of trail with two other hikers. I kept my mouth shut as I heard them proudly point out that they'd be carrying seven days' worth of food for the first time. Their eyes and tone told us that seven days was so crazy that anything longer just wasn't possible. We had just carried ten days' worth from Cabazon to Agua Dulce, and were going to carry at least ten more all the way to

Kennedy Meadows. I didn't want to crush their egos, but I also didn't want to hear them tell us we couldn't do it.

It's not a resupply strategy that I would recommend to most, nor am I sure I would do it again. But, it worked well for Optimist and me, which made it all the more frustrating when others told us we were living that part of the trail wrong. We built a piece of the puzzle that worked for us, and we could have cared less if anyone else tried fitting that piece into their own puzzle. All we asked was that others let us continue to build our own as long as our building didn't detrimentally affect their own. Instead, other hikers would look at our puzzle and recommend a piece that didn't fit. Even if it could have been molded to fit, they never gave us a reason why the piece they were suggesting was better than the one we'd already made. We spent a lot of effort molding our own pieces, and we weren't about to throw them out because they fit the majority of puzzles so poorly.

One consequence of only resupplying in towns within a mile of the trail was that we ended up missing out on A LOT of towns. We could have been in a town every three to five days if we had wanted, carrying much less food and basking in the glory of many more pizzas. But, we made the choice to stick to the trail as our main residence.

There was a gauntlet of towns in California within the first five hundred miles, such as Warner Springs, Idyllwild, Big Bear, and Wrightwood. I'm sure they are all great towns. But, the towns became a spider web for thru-hikers. Once they were lured in, they got stuck and couldn't seem to leave. It gets harder and harder to get back on the trail the more time that is spent in the luxury of a town. Towns have food, showers, laundry, and beds…every piece of a comfortable life indoors that becomes magnetic once you've spent an extended period of time living outside.

The towns were every bit magnetic to Optimist and me as they were to other thru-hikers. We simply avoided them. We also didn't miss out on any experience that wasn't filled by an even better one around the campfire with other thru-hikers on the trail. For us, the point of thru-hiking the PCT was to experience the lifestyle of living on a trail for several months. It was a lifestyle that we felt privileged to live. Not many people can leave the real world for four months while they walk over 2600 miles. There were a lot of factors that had to align to allow for a thru-hike, and the summer of 2007 was it. We hadn't had the chance to do it before, and didn't know when we would afterwards. We wanted to make the most of every moment spent together on the trail. Towns would always be there.

There are two very different town lifestyles, and the one we chose was best for us. Our PCT lifestyle wasn't that of spending most of our time in towns with a little side time on the trail in order to get to the next town. It was that of fully living in the outdoor world, but needing town stops to allow us to continue the outdoor time. If we had lived the first lifestyle, I'm afraid I would have never started the trail or gotten back on it after my first town stop.

Many people thought we were crazy for skipping so many towns, many were downright angry with us, and many thought we were depriving ourselves of the true trail experience. What many people didn't take into account was that we were forming our own unique trail experience, carving our own niche, and guiding our own lifestyle as thru-hikers. We found that we were able to get in a much better rhythm by skipping towns because we weren't rushing to finish by 5:00 p.m. to make the post office hours, we spent much less money, and we were never lured to take many rest days. We never once paid for lodging on the entire trail. It is a cost that can add up and deplete trail funds quickly. A big reason people never make it to Canada is because they run out of money, and it's not from buying too much Top Ramen.

If we had hit more towns in the beginning, I would not have stuck with the trail. It was hard enough getting back on the trail after leaving the towns we *did* visit. I can't imagine tripling the number of times that I felt the exciting yet exhausting town pull. Towns truly are magnetic, and crazy Stopwatch would come out in anticipation of town-time. Upon leaving towns, I always had to deal with the tiring feeling of getting back on the trail with a full stomach and a lack of motivation to walk. It took me a long time to admit to myself that I was better off living most of my time on the trail, and that the experience that would benefit me the most was laid out before me on the long brown ribbon of the trail rather than on a black asphalt road through town.

When we skipped a town, simply by crossing a road rather than hitching a ride down it, we inevitably ran into other hikers going into or coming out of town. The ones going in would show disbelief as we waved them goodbye. We knew we'd most likely never see them again if they planned on taking a day off while we moved another twenty-five to thirty miles up the trail. The ones coming out of town would recount stories of food, soft beds, and warm showers. All of them would wonder why we would voluntarily miss out on the best rumored pizza, bakery or milkshakes along the entire trail.

We knew that while they may be right, that we were missing out on creature comforts, we weren't missing anything we couldn't experience once we finished the trail. There would always be pizza and ice cream, but there might not always be a trail. We couldn't experience more trail once we were at the Canadian border. Instead, we tried to soak up that time as much as possible. That said, I'd be lying if I said I wasn't jealous a few times upon seeing their clean clothes, swollen mid-sections, and well-polished skin.

Perhaps even another result of long resupplies, coupled with skipping towns, was that there were fewer opportunities to take zero days. Zero days are when the hiking shoes are hung up for a full day and zero trail miles are recorded in the books. Usually, an entire day is spent resting and eating in town.

Optimist and I did not take a single zero day along the entire trail. We hiked every day of our 109 days on the trail.

We did take a few nero days, or days when few miles were recorded. They were near a zero, but not quite, as we still walked more than zero miles. We hiked just two days that were six and eight miles each. Otherwise, there was not a day on the trail that was below six miles, and about seven days were below fifteen miles.

Just as we had not planned on our food resupply strategy that was so radically different from others', we had no intentions of not taking any zero days while planning for the trail, or even after we had started hiking. Before we started, zero days were the lore of the trail. They were a part of the trail I looked forward to experiencing first hand. I imagined myself kicking back on the side of a pool, feeding on ice cream while my clothes tumbled in a washer and dryer nearby. I had listened to enough stories of Optimist, Rocketcop, and Animal's zero days from the Appalachian Trail to know that I would thoroughly enjoy them.

The seed was planted for a zero-dayless trail on day twenty-one, upon reaching Agua Dulce. We hadn't taken a zero day yet, and didn't intend on taking one in Agua Dulce. We had hiked an easy eighteen miles into town that day, arriving by 1:00 p.m. We left ourselves plenty of time to indulge for the afternoon, evening and next morning, with plans to start hiking the next afternoon.

When one of the trail angels in town found out that we wouldn't be taking a zero day the next day, she was a little put off, and quickly advised, "Even elite athletes take days off."

Her perceivable annoyance at our actions took us off guard. We didn't know it was customary for thru-hikers to take a zero in Agua Dulce. We just knew that we were hiking well, that we didn't feel tired or injured, and that we felt it was ample time off from 1:00 p.m. one day to around 1:00 p.m. the next day. We weren't denying ourselves of a zero day because we were afraid of getting behind in mileage. We simply didn't feel like we needed a day off. Luckily, the lifestyle of long-distance backpacking was fitting for us. We were good at covering miles for days at a time, and we simply enjoyed living outside together. Every day before the start of the trail and every day after the completion of the trail was a zero day, so why take them on the trail if we didn't need them?

This was an incredibly hard concept for so many other thru-hikers and trail angels. They would look at us with cold eyes that accused us of lying, of hiding some other motive for not taking days off. Most thought we were hiking with a deadline, but our calendar was wide open after the trail. We didn't have jobs lined up, let alone an established place to live. The trail really was our home at the time, and we planned on figuring out our next steps while we literally took our next steps.

Within the first ten days of our hike, before we had met many other thru-hikers, we had the pleasure of crossing paths with a well-known trail legend, Tatu-Jo. He has thru-hiked the trail more times than is healthy to speak of, and has set the speed record for hiking it in the fewest amount of days. Tatu set the speed record the year we hiked it. He finished it in seventy-nine days. Divide 2663 miles by seventy-nine days and you'll get a pretty high daily average of miles. That doesn't even count his zero days, of which I knew he had at least five. And people said we hiked crazy miles.

Despite our vast differences, we got along well with Tatu. He was an ultralight hiker whose pack weighed around fifteen pounds, who frequently stopped in towns to avoid long resupplies, and who hiked fast miles. We were Team Sherpa, the name given by Tatu himself, our packs were overloaded with food, we didn't stop in many towns, and we hiked slow miles. We only covered a lot of miles because we hiked all day. Everything about our way of hiking versus Tatu's should have driven a rift between us and him. We should have never gotten along.

The difference in our relationship with Tatu versus that with other hikers was that even though neither side wanted to emulate the other side's way of hiking, each could respect the other side for doing it their way and still making it on the trail. Each of us could see pros and cons of the different ways of hiking, and each of us was willing to listen to advice from the other side, just in case there was some validity that made the other side's way worth trying.

The other difference in Tatu from other hikers was that he was confident in his process, in his methods, and was in no way threatened by us. We were complete newbies to the PCT, trying to carve our own niche and go our own way. He was downright tickled by our success in moving up the trail rather quickly and in good health despite our unconventional methods of long-distance backpacking, which stood as a polar opposite from his own.

After knowing us for several days, Tatu gave us a piece of advice that stuck with us for the rest of the trail. He had hiked the trail so many times and met so many people along the way, year after year. He had often hiked such high mileage that he was used to the skeptics, the ones that told him he was hiking it all wrong. He was accustomed to people telling him that he was hiking too fast, that he wasn't enjoying the experience, and that he wasn't stopping to see the views or smell the flowers.

Tatu knew of our unconventional hiking methods. He knew what we were in for. Up to that point, we hadn't seen the *real* pack of other thru-hikers. We'd only met late starters, and hadn't met too much resistance from others as we defined our way of hiking. Tatu had met so many people that were quick to judge his own style that he warned us, "If you're going to hike this way, be ready for people to not like you. There are plenty of people who will tell you you're doing it wrong."

We quickly shrugged off his advice and thought he was over exaggerating, that he was being his quirky Tatu self, that he'd met more bad apples than we had. But he was exactly right. What seemed like an unlikely reaction from other hikers became more of the norm along the way as people learned what kind of mileage we hiked and what kind of town strategies we'd implemented. It was the strangest phenomenon that people should actually care about our methods, and care so much that they had the confidence in their own methods to tell us we were doing it all wrong. I had heard the "hike your own hike" advice so often, but wondered if others actually believed it, or if they added on the caveat, "As long as it's not too different from my own hike."

Another large piece of Optimist's and my PCT puzzle was the ability to avoid the temptation of the herd.

The herd represented the main pack of hikers that started in mid to late April. They traveled together in large groups up the trail and through trail towns. We saw their names in the trail journals along the way as we made our way north. We knew who was ahead of us and how close they were to each other. People usually wrote the date and their name, and sometimes even the time, so it was easy to see groups moving together.

The herd is a nice place to be. It's comforting to be around other people in unfamiliar situations, which is pretty much the entire trail. Every step taken brings forth new experiences, different terrain, varied scenery, unexpected weather, and unique towns. The herd is safety in numbers. It means group decisions in lieu of individual ones. It is a piece of civilization while out on the wild, free trail.

The herd is also dangerous. The more time spent in the herd, the harder it becomes to have alone time. Experiences are defined by how they affect the group rather than the individual. The ability to change the course of decisions becomes quite difficult once the herd is put in motion. The herd also causes a person to doubt his ability to make it on his own once he's been in it for a stretch of time.

The longer in it, the harder it becomes to leave it. It also may make group decisions that a hiker would have otherwise not made if left up only to that individual. Once swept into the herd mentality, it becomes harder to uphold individual values. The herd makes it harder to hike your own hike.

Lastly, the herd is a bit destructive as it moves up the trail and through trail towns. It moves in like a tornado and takes over all resources for the span of its stay. Every single night on the trail is a new place to call home, so imagine droves of new people moving in to a new place each night on a patch of land or in the main street of a small town. The group sets up tents, builds fires, books hotel rooms and fills up restaurants. It becomes a bit more difficult to "leave no trace" when group sizes number upwards of twenty people or more.

Optimist and I camped with others at times just like the herd, though we still had plenty of nights with just ourselves. Contrary to the herd, every decision we made was of our own thoughts and weighing. We never once felt pressured to act simply because it was what other hikers did. We were also never afraid to simply go our own way, even if it meant alienation from the herd.

Early in the Central California section is Mt. Whitney, the highest point in the Continental US. It is reached via a side trail off the PCT. The majority of thru-hikers take the opportunity to hike to the top of Mt. Whitney, knowing they may never have the chance to be there again in their lifetime.

Optimist and I decided to pass up Mt. Whitney. We didn't want to hike any more miles than was necessary. We were there to walk the PCT, and weren't interested in side trails, even if they led to monumental locations. I don't feel as if we missed out by not hiking to the top of Mt. Whitney, but I did feel the tension from other hikers as we revealed our decision to opt out of the side trip. Other thru-hikers were openly angry and annoyed at our decision and tried to sway us to change our course. The more we told people that we weren't hiking it, the more annoyed *I* got with their reactions. It seemed so strange to me that other people cared about our decision to hike to a mountaintop.

It was an experience almost every other thru-hiker had, so why wouldn't we want that?

Because it was ultimately our decision to hike whatever extra miles we wanted, because our only concerns were the PCT miles, because we were willing to deal with whatever consequences our decisions led to, and because they were our decisions and no one else's.

While we were a part of the herd in the bigger picture, being thru-hikers just as they were, we were different enough to be outside the herd in the smaller picture. We mingled with the herd on the fringe, but were cautious, for fear of losing our individuality and our ability to choose.

Another section that drew forth differences between us and others was just before the town of Cascade Locks, Oregon, on the border between Oregon and Washington. Many thru-hikers skip the section in lieu of another trail, the Eagle Creek Trail. It gets you to Cascade Locks just as the PCT does, but it's a more scenic trail. Many hikers take that route mainly because a bit of boredom has set in at that point. It's something new and exciting, and it does cut some mileage from the trail.

Since it's not officially the PCT, Optimist and I stuck with the same PCT trail we'd hiked for over 2100 miles up to that point. Some called us "purists", a negative connotation in their tone, which I can't disagree with.

All I can say is that we set out to hike from Mexico to Canada on the PCT, so why take trails that are not the PCT in order to get there? If that made us purists, then so be it. We didn't care about others taking a different trail to get to the same end point. All we wanted was to be able to hike our own hike without getting slack from others that we were following the trail too closely. We had set out on a journey that only follows one trail in the first place. We were some of the few hikers to hike the real PCT into Cascade Locks. The trail didn't show as much wear as other parts, and the scenery wasn't that great once we left the stunning views of the Columbia River Gorge and dropped down into the long descent full of switchbacks and stifled views through the trees. We also cleared quite a bit of spider webs. Few people had cleared the webs before us, and I doubt many cleared them afterwards. The irony is that I live about forty-five minutes from the Eagle Creek Trail today. I can enjoy it any time I want. Of course, Optimist and I didn't know at the time when we skipped Eagle Creek that we would someday live so close to it. Regardless of that outcome, we went our own way, which was just the plain vanilla PCT.

Though Optimist and I disagreed with the way the others were hiking, taking short cuts, avoiding actually walking on the PCT, there was never a moment where we told them how to hike, where we told them they were doing it "wrong." We simply knew that their way was wrong for us, and that our way was right for us, and left it at that. Again, it created tension between us and the other hikers because we exuded our pride in sticking to the PCT the entire way, in never wavering from its path.

How else could we honestly say to ourselves and to others that we thru-hiked the Pacific Crest Trail if we hadn't actually stuck to the trail the entire way? What's the point of staking claim to a thru-hike if you don't hike all its miles? Even if the herd takes a shortcut as a group, does that bring you any closer to being a thru-hiker just because everyone agreed on the shortcut being acceptable? In our minds, the herd's decisions were never justified on the premises of many people making the same choice. The herd merely took the decisions away from individuals. While it made decisions easier for individuals because less thought had to be put into the decision, the herd also took away the ability of hikers to make their own unique experience.

Many people may not like this, but I think hikers were jealous that we made our own personal brand of long-distance backpacking. We had created a Team Sherpa way of hiking that suited us well, despite being vastly different from the norm. I think it downright scared people that such a different way could be possible. Most others couldn't help but follow a common way of thru-hiking: getting stuck in the web of towns, spending too much money, taking too many zeros, and having a hard time covering the miles when a town was always pulling on them, whether coming in or leaving.

Optimist and I were also proud of our feats, and perhaps that pride was worn too outwardly on our faces, our demeanor, and our tone. Other hikers that were prone to being insecure with their way of doing things probably didn't appreciate our pride in doing it our own way. It was so foreign to their own way. We could have cared less how other hikers molded their experience, but took offense when others would tell us that we were doing it all wrong, that we were missing out by not taking days off, that we were hiking too fast to truly enjoy the trail. If anyone ever actually hiked with us, they would have found my pace painfully slow.

There were times where Optimist and I saw that the herd was detrimental to individual hikers. One particular couple sticks out in our minds, Hitch and Cabana Boy. We met them at Virginia Lake, two nights before reaching Tuolumne Meadows in Yosemite National Park in California.

The night at Virginia Lake was crowded. It was probably the largest group, at least twenty people, which we stayed with along the entire trail. Optimist and I were hiking fairly fast through Central California at that point. We were catching more and more of the herd each day, moving through and beyond the pack as people peeled off for towns along the way. We caught a huge group that evening at Virginia Lake. Nearly the entire group was going to the town of Mammoth Lakes the next day, a popular resting town for hikers. We planned on skipping the town and continuing up the trail, our sights set on Tuolumne Meadows. Our food was dwindling quickly, as was our body weight. All we cared about were the boxes of food we knew were awaiting us at Tuolumne Meadows.

We gained useful insights into the herd that evening, listening to stories of all the names in the journals that we'd seen the whole way up the trail. We watched all of them take their place among the large group's small groupings, and we heard plans of everyone's next few days. It was the first evening that we saw the herd in action, camping together over a large area of ground, sharing stories together, building several campfires together, and planning the next day's hike and town stop.

While it felt nice at first to Optimist and me, to have company again at camp, it felt suffocating. It felt like we had planted our living room party out there on the trail, the only difference being that we were hungrier and dirtier than we would have otherwise been at a party.

We were also quite an anomaly to the other hikers. Having started later and having molded our own brand of thru-hiking, we had had such a different experience thus far from all the others. Our ways were vastly different from others'. We were prepared to be snuffed, inevitably making enemies just as easily as friends, so we kept fairly quiet about how differently we were hiking the trail from those surrounding us. While some admired our way of hiking, a lot simply didn't want to hear about it.

Hitch and Cabana Boy were two hikers that we befriended the next day. They had planned on joining the herd into Mammoth Lakes, but changed their minds when they heard we were moving on. A new way of hiking had been presented to them, and so they tried it. We hiked into the evening with them, our headlamps guiding our way. The possibilities for conversation among us seemed endless as we walked under the moonlight. I didn't want to stop walking, because that meant the conversation would inevitably end. Once our bodies were horizontal, sleep quickly took over.

Our new-found friends had hiked with a group the entire way, and weren't having an easy time in making their way up the trail. By the time we met them, they were making a list of pros and cons for staying on the trail. This meant that the cons must have been weighing pretty heavily beyond their pros. I didn't have a good feeling about their odds, as it was the first attempt at a thru-hike for both of them. But, I was hopeful they would see that in us creating our own brand of hiking, we made our experience more enjoyable. I wanted them to see that they didn't need to herd to get them to Canada, that they could create their own brand of hiking as well. They could still be confident in their own decisions, even if someone laid a seed of doubt in their minds about their way of doing things. I wanted them to look at what benefited them and not just the herd.

Hitch and Cabana Boy did not make it further than the next day at Tuolumne Meadows. The last we saw of them, they were sitting at a picnic table in front of the general store, debating whether to stay on the trail or get off and call it a good try. It was difficult leaving them, knowing what decision they were leaning towards, knowing that we couldn't make the decision for them. We would have been no better than the herd in making that decision. Still, we would have told them to walk away with us from the store, to keep going on the trail. We knew the odds of seeing them again were slim once we left them to their own doubting minds.

Optimist and I questioned how their experience would have been different had they been able to create a separate entity of themselves aside from the herd. Would they have made it had they spent more time making decisions that only affected them? Would more alone time on the trail have helped, or more time with just each other?

It's impossible to say, but I believe that Hitch and Cabana Boy's odds of finishing would have been greatly increased had they learned early on that it's ok to avoid the herd. In no way would I have wanted them to adopt a lifestyle along the trail that would have negatively affected the herd, as that's no better than the opposite. I would have advised them to take a hard look at what they needed to do as individuals and as a couple to make it to Canada. I imagine that with keeping the end goal of reaching the border, they would have enjoyed the experience all the while, knowing that it was their own choices that got them there.

The end result of Optimist and I hiking our own hike, of avoiding the temptation of the herd, was that we had to deal with the consequences of our actions. We had to deal with not being liked or accepted by others because of our chosen lifestyle on the PCT. It's easier said than done to feel ok with not being liked, with being seen as the fringe of the pack. It's like being labeled as a nerd in high school. Sure, you know that those people's opinions of you don't matter, and that they will fade once you've started real life. That being said, it still sucks to be pigeonholed as a nerd, no matter how cool you are otherwise. And at that age, it just doesn't cut it if only your mom thinks you're cool.

Optimist and I certainly felt the fuzz of the fringe and the tension in the air as we caught up with other hikers and then passed them. Once people learned of our different ways of putting together important pieces of the trail puzzle, they were either intrigued, eager to hear more, or downright annoyed that we were getting away with such a unique way of life. It was usually easy to tell upon meeting other hikers, who would accept our way of life, even if they didn't agree with it, or who would avoid much conversation and hurry to zip the tent door shut.

While it was difficult at first, being told we were doing it wrong before we even started the trail, it actually helped our confidence the more people assured us our way was wrong. It only added more fuel to our fire, more drive in our legs, to want to prove others wrong. We could also deal with others not liking us simply because at the beginning and end of each day, it boiled down to Optimist and me. All we really had to face was each other and our own selves. As long as we still loved each other through the entire process, it didn't matter that others felt aversion towards us. There were still plenty that didn't, and we found those types of people extremely enjoyable to be around. The quantity of people who found us agreeable didn't matter. It was the quality of people who enjoyed our company that was a highlight along the trail.

Learning this lesson and putting it into practice outside of the trail has been invaluable to both me and Optimist. "Hike your own Hike" could just as well be titled, "Live your own Life." Look around and it's easy to see that there is no one way to live a life. If there were, how boring would that be? Part of the excitement of life is knowing that our lives are our own to mold, to shape, and to change. We're able to choose our own path, to be ok with going our own way, even if it means being far off course from the norm. As long as our course does not lead to a path of destruction for other peoples' courses, the greater good could benefit from the individuals being given the freedom to create the most enjoyable, fulfilled lives. I hope we never lose the freedom to choose how to live.

I've learned to be wary of people that tell me I'm doing it all wrong, that I'm making the wrong life decisions, and that I'm not on the "right" path, as if its existence is proven. I've come to believe that the correct life path is found at the bottom of the lake where the Loch Nest Monster lives. Rumors of its existence have been tossed around, but has anyone actually seen it? Has anyone actually proven that there is a right path to follow in life?

Optimist and I keep life pretty simple. We don't have cable, our cell phones are the free ones that came with the plan, we lived together for seven years before marrying, and our wedding was drastically different from anything we've ever attended. The list goes on as to how we do things differently in our everyday lives. The list of skeptics continues on even further than that. We've had many people tell us how we should be living, which is often much closer to their own way of life.

Now that we've gained confidence in our way of life due to the trail and other life changing experiences, we've come to wonder if people question our way of living because they question their own. They have no firm platform on which they've based their life values and beliefs. They only have the norm to reference, and deep down, they wonder if their way is even good for themselves, let alone others. It's rare that those same people have good reasons for us to live their own way. If someone can convince us that their way of life is in fact better than what we're implementing now, by way of reasoning and logic rather than by emotions and unfounded claims, we're open to possibilities of going down their suggested path. But if others want us to change our course simply because it's so vastly different from their own, because their lack of confidence in their course entails that we should equally lack confidence in ours, we'll kindly step back and remind them that while we're letting them hike their own hike, we ask that they do the same for us.

10 YOU HAVE A CHOICE

There are many moments from the trail that I'm proud to share with others. I will shout them from the mountaintops and go on record with them. On the flip side, there are just as many moments that I'm not proud of and that I hesitate to divulge. I'm talking about the moments where I was misbehaving, having a tantrum, having a mental breakdown and trying to drag Optimist down with me. Moments where I'm surprised the trail didn't open up right in front of me and swallow me whole, not allowing me to come back up for air until I promised to have a more positive attitude and to appreciate the trail for all its beauty and grandeur. Maybe the trail should have done that, as I may have learned this lesson much earlier. It took me the entire length of the trail to realize that I ultimately have a choice when it comes to my happiness.

The trail was an emotional roller coaster for me. I could be so high with happiness from reaching a town or completing a section, but then I could be so low with frustration in the difficulty of the hike and a lack of desire to continue. It was a constant up and down, a love/hate relationship with both me and the trail.

Sometimes the smallest event, such as tripping over a rock, would set me into a spiral of tears and hyperventilating. I would get angry at the trail and grab the rock that I just tripped over, throw it off the side of the trail, screaming profanities and hurling my crazed madness with it. Rather than be angry at myself for not picking up my lazy feet and legs, I would actually get mad at both the trail and the rock, the trail because of its existence, and the rock because it got in my way. It may seem silly, but these were my reactions to my clumsiness and lack of adeptness in hiking over rocks and logs and any other obstructions found along the trail. What I didn't realize was that the rocks, the logs, and the trail itself, were all in existence long before I decided to show up. I was actually infringing on their natural habitat, so it was my job to make sure *my* presence didn't interfere with their position. I was a guest in their home, and I treated the host like an ungrateful brat.

I'm almost ashamed of those moments of misbehavior when I reflect back on them. The only reason I'm willing to admit them is because I have actually learned important lessons from them. I have learned that I'm choosing to react negatively to situations, that I'm blaming outside factors for my own shortcomings, and that I still have a choice regarding my own happiness. In my mind, the lesson of choosing happiness is the hardest lesson to fully see and to fully realize its worth and ability to extend to every part of life. Choosing happiness involves taking a step back from the details directly in front of us in order to see the picture as a whole. The details of the trail that clouded my vision and added to the stress were the hunger, the thirst, the exhaustion, and even my own self. I had a difficult time stepping back from those obstacles in order to see the greater picture of the trail itself and my reactions to all its pieces. The times when I was able to pause for a moment and get my head out of the details were my shining moments. They were the moments I found it easiest to choose happiness.

Choosing happiness is the hardest lesson to practice with any sort of consistency. This explains why my emotions rode the roller coaster so often on the trail and even in real life today. Once the minute details were right in front of my eyes, knee-jerk reactions happened rather than thought-out, self-reflective ones. My initial reaction to a negative situation was rarely, if ever, to choose to be happy. Stressors from the trail are just like all the pieces of life that constantly surround us like our own personal tornadoes, threatening to gather strength and speed in order to rip us apart from the inside. We are surrounded by to-do lists, bills and deadlines that will never really leave our sides. But, the stressors can't rip us apart by their own existence. We choose to let them.

The way I received my trail name, Stopwatch, exemplifies my behavior on the trail. My name was mostly self-named, but those around me at the time were in thorough agreement with the choice.

Early on in the trail, I constantly looked at the data book. It held all the mileage information, so I often calculated how long each section should take us, estimating fifteen to twenty minutes for each mile. I used these numbers and figured out when I thought we should arrive at key points, like a water source or a road.

There were sections that simply took longer than expected, usually because of a tough uphill or tired legs. I was in denial of this fact. On the third day, we came upon a creek that I thought would be the one I was looking forward to in the book. It was in fact the previous creek that I thought we'd already passed. We'd gone at least a mile and a half less than I thought. We still had much further to go, and the realization made my stomach drop and my blood boil. I was pissed. I stopped walking, threw down my pack and yelled at Optimist, "We should have been there by now! How have we only walked three miles in that time?"

I can still see Optimist's face of shock and disgust.

Thus the name Stopwatch was born. I was obsessed with the watch, the timing of the miles, and the estimation of our arrival times. My name was given and my watch was taken away that same day. The next day, the data book was taken away from me too. Optimist had had enough of my obsessive timing of the miles and carried both items in his pack from then on.

I willingly gave both of them up. My head hung in defeat from trying to control the trail and plan out each day's hike. I was driving not only myself mad, but Optimist too. Neither of us could have made it the entire way had I kept up my bad habits. I would have gone crazy, a blubbering mess, only able to yell, "We should have been there by now!" Or Optimist would have had to take leave of me, not able to enjoy his own trail experience while I threatened to ruin it with each passing data point.

I did earn my watch back eventually, on day fifty, only after good behavior and a promise to not time the miles. I never earned the book back.

One reason I never earned the data book back was because of a special little feature called the gradient. The gradient column in the book tells how big or small the next hill will be for a given section. A gradient number like −1.2 for a mile means that it's a slight downhill for that mile, and a number like 3.4 for a mile means it's a decent uphill. The bigger the number, the steeper the up or down. The gradients were only true to their numbers if they referred to a small

135

mileage point, such as a mile or less. There were times when we walked long stretches without a landmark, such as three to five miles, where the gradient could not be trusted. It could be a roller coaster through a five-mile section for all we knew, beginning and ending at the same elevation, but making us climb and descend unforgiving terrain in between. This was incredibly hard for me to swallow. If the book marked a zero gradient, that meant the section must be flat, right? No, no, no…that thinking got me in big trouble.

Unfortunately, my photographic memory would allow me to memorize almost an entire page of the book at a time. Even though Optimist only let me peak at it a couple of times a day, I always knew in my head what was coming. He would catch me cursing at an uphill, mumbling under my breath, "Stupid negative gradient. I thought this was supposed to be a downhill! What are we doing going up?"

It was as if I *wanted* the self-torture. Once Optimist realized that I was memorizing landmarks and gradients between sections, feverishly scanning the data book, he would swipe it out of my hands and threaten to never let me view it again. He at least never let me carry it again.

The more I memorized gradients, wishing for them to be true to their numbers, the more negative I became. I replaced the obsession with the stopwatch with the obsession with the hills. An uphill climb or a false gradient grew into feeling like the trail had a personal vendetta against me, like it steepened its hills just for me because it knew how much I craved flat ground. All I wanted was for the hiking to be easier, and the key to that was a flat trail. Optimist would often remind me that the trail traversed mountains, not meadows.

Amazingly, especially now that I look back on it, I would actually get angry at the trail for going uphill, sighing in disgust as I looked up to face the trail climbing to great heights above me, switchbacks awaiting me. It was as if the trail was a real person to me. I later realized that I was creating all the drama between the trail and myself. It was all a play in my mind, with me cast as the main protagonist, and my worst enemy being the trail. I treated the trail as if it had a personality, but the fact was that the trail was an inanimate object that was there before me and that would be there when I left. I was not so special that the trail would shape itself specifically for my own mental and physical anguish.

I also learned to accept the fact that I was full of myself and creating my own unhappiness. I was taking an act that was so simple, walking, and turning it into a soap opera in my head. I cried in defeat and yelled in anger because I couldn't handle the act of putting one foot in front of the other. The trail never had it in for me. All I had to do was walk and deal with whatever was ahead of me, knowing to expect the unexpected. Looking back, I'm surprised there weren't trail police ready to kick me off the trail for bad behavior.

Aside from my snippets of insanity, there were my own personal mental breakdowns. I'm least proud of those moments. They were moments when I blamed everyone else for my unhappiness, when I was ready to throw in the towel, to end the trail, to end my relationship with Optimist, and to give up because it was just too darn hard. Those moments would hit me hard, punch me in the stomach, and double me over in pain, anguish, and loads of tears. I could feel them coming like a storm rolling in overhead. As my negativity gained momentum, the mental breakdowns gained in strength and speed, promising a relapse in positive steps forward. After the first few, Optimist learned the signs of them, choosing to walk ahead without me and let me deal with them alone. Only I caused them, so only I could fix them. At first I was angry that he didn't help me through them or comfort me in my tears, but then I was glad that he didn't witness my lashing out at myself and the trail. I didn't want him in the path of my anger, as I was sure to direct it towards him.

In addition to the many mini-mental lapses where negativity would overwhelm me for short periods of time, I had five specific breakdowns along the trail. Each one left more space between the next as I learned to deal with them better. I accepted that they happened, I got through them after thinking things over in my own head, and I learned from each one of them.

The first mental breakdown was on day nine. I let my negative attitude blind me in the San Jacinto Mountains in Southern California. It had been a hard climb that morning (mental breakdowns usually involved a climb). Optimist and I were hiking with Rocketcop and Prozac, and at the time, it seemed like everyone around me was enjoying the experience and having no trouble in making it up the seemingly endless, steep uphill. Now that I look back on it, I see that everyone was struggling with the climb just as I was. Since I couldn't see past my own self, I never stopped to think about what the others might have been going through.

There was a moment that morning where we all decided to take a break on the climb. There was an inviting outcropping of boulders off the side of the trail, just asking for us to sit on them.

Rocketcop, Prozac and Optimist all chose boulders within a few feet of each other. I purposely sat about ten feet away from the group, not wanting to converse with anyone. The only thoughts going through my mind were, "How do I get off this trail? How do I quit? Why am I doing this?"

I didn't have an answer to any of my questions. I'd never known myself to quit a challenge, yet I couldn't fully explain why I was even trying. I was overwhelmed by the vast amount of miles ahead and especially overwhelmed by just how difficult hiking was, both physically and mentally.

I sat on my rock and stared off into the green and brown backdrop that was our stage as the group enjoyed the break. They must have known that the wheels of self-doubt were turning in my head. My face showed it; it was a look that was hard to mask. I was barely holding it together as we all sat in near silence. After Rocketcop and Prozac continued on, Optimist sat next to me and asked why I looked so sad, as if he really had to guess. I couldn't hold in my tears of defeat and disappointment any longer. I became a blubbering mess, blurting out phrases like, "I can't," and "I'm getting off the trail," between my streaming tears. It was the first time I vocalized my craving to get off the trail, and I dumped it all on Optimist as he sat there in silence. For at least ten minutes, I cried and listed the reasons for my unhappiness and desire to end the trail.

Optimist wasn't very consoling. He certainly listened to me choke on my words, as my throat closed up with anxiety. After a while he let me know that while he preferred I stay on the trail with him, he'd continue the trail no matter what my decision would be. It was a dose of reality that I wasn't expecting to come so coldly from Optimist, but perhaps I needed it. I realized that ending the trail might be the end of Optimist and me. We had been together for more than four years, so it felt wrong to let something as simple as a trail end us. I promised myself to at least give it a few more days before I considered quitting again.

I still wanted to quit many times after that first mental breakdown, but the mental lapse led to me to see that it was ultimately my choice to be on the trail. It was my choice as to whether I was going to put forth my best effort to enjoy the experience. Optimist may have preferred me to join him, but he couldn't decide for me to stay on the trail, just as he couldn't decide for me to be happy. That part was up to me, and many times along the trail, I failed miserably at making that state of mind a reality.

The next two mental breakdowns fortunately did not happen for another few weeks, but unfortunately happened two days in a row. It was a double whammy, one-two punch of mental breakdowns, where I was more tired from the tears and riding the emotional roller coaster than I was from hiking.

The Central California section of the trail was the most physically challenging section for Optimist and me. It had big climbs and big descents. The terrain was much more difficult than we had expected, and it was cooler in the evenings. We expended far more energy than we had planned for, both while we were moving and while we were sleeping. That combination meant our bodies were burning a crazy amount of calories, yet we didn't have enough food to replace those calories. We had to ration food the entire way, which inevitably meant our bodies shed pounds. Weight loss sounds like a great problem to have, but when a grocery store is nowhere in sight, exhaustion and hunger take their toll on both the mind and body.

In that difficult section were the towns of Reds Meadows and Tuolumne Meadows. Reds Meadows had a small general store and a restaurant rumored for pie and milkshakes. On the day into Reds Meadows, we only had fifteen miles to walk to reach it. That morning, my only goal was to make it to Reds Meadows. I was so focused on the upcoming smorgasbord of food that I didn't want to stop for any breaks, not even breakfast or lunch. I wanted to only eat trail mix or energy bars while I walked in order to get in the miles as quickly as possible.

After about six miles, that plan crumbled. We'd been walking for a couple of hours and I could not go for another few hours without any fuel in me. I started to get myself worked up in a vicious cycle of negative thoughts that swirled in my head. All I could think of was how difficult the hike was, how much I didn't want to be there, and how much I just wanted to be doing normal things. I wanted to wake up in a bed, with coffee brewing while I showered and dressed for a day at the office. The life that I knew so many of my friends were living seemed like a life made in heaven, and I wanted it so much more than the life I was having at that moment.

I was at a low point that morning. I grumbled profanities and phrases of anger under my breath and wouldn't talk to Optimist. I was only focused on the task at hand, arriving at Reds Meadows for milkshakes. He followed me silently, not wanting to say anything that might bring on the wrath of another mental breakdown.

It wasn't until we ran into a weekend hiker that I realized just how pervasive my negativity was that morning. It was so thick that even a stranger knew when he walked into my cloud of anger.

As Optimist and I reached the top of a small hill, we saw another hiker sitting on a log off the side of the trail, just finishing lacing up his boots. I had a scowl on my face as we walked closer to him.

Optimist introduced himself first. He was always happy to meet someone new.

"Hi, I'm Optimist!"

"Nice to meet you," the hiker said. After turning to me and looking me over for a brief moment, he said, "And you must be Pessimist."

Optimist found it funny, but since I was already in a wretched mood, it only set me off further. I snipped out a "Hah" and walked away as Optimist and he walked behind me and chatted for the next mile. Our new acquaintance made my head spin with new thoughts.

What upset me, more than the hiker calling me a pessimist, was that he could read me that quickly, within seconds of meeting me. I carried around that much negativity on my face and through my body language that a complete stranger could know to steer clear of my mood without me even saying a word.

If I looked that upset to strangers, what did I look like to Optimist? Did he think I downright hated the experience and was hanging on for dear life because I thought it would make him happy that I got through the experience? Surely, Optimist's experience wasn't enhanced at all by sensing that I was miserable and only attempting the thru-hike to make him happy. It wasn't up to him whether I was happy, and it wasn't up to me if he was happy. We were on our own at figuring that out, and I was undoubtedly failing at holding up my side of the bargain.

After about twenty minutes, I couldn't take the hunger or the exhaustion any longer. I started crying as I asked Optimist if we would stop and eat a cooked breakfast rather than pushing through the miles. I was losing it quickly, and he was happy to oblige. He was just as hungry as I was, and tired of trying to go without a meal for fifteen miles.

As we sat there and waited for the noodles to boil, I took a deeper look at myself. It hit me that while Optimist remained focused on the moment, all I wanted to do was get through the moment without taking in any of it. I was always hoping the next moment would be better. Yet every time I actually reached the highly-awaited moment, disappointment would set in because the moment was no more special than the last.

That morning, I freed myself from the town-pull of Reds Meadows. I told myself that we'd get there when we got there, that the food would be there whether I got there in two hours or four, and that the only goal wasn't just to arrive at a place. I no longer wanted a stranger to be able to call me a pessimist and to be so right in his presumptions. I wanted to look like I belonged with Optimist. Rather than drag him down in my negativity, I wanted to help lift both of our spirits by working on lifting my own.

I can't say that I figured it all out that morning. I knew that I couldn't continue the trail in the same state of mind that had led me through it thus far, but I couldn't quite pinpoint how to equate my attitude with a more enjoyable experience. I didn't know how to make my own happiness while I was still clawing myself out of the black hole of negativity.

Amazingly, just like the movie *Groundhog Day*, I woke up the next morning and repeated the entire process all over again. My self-reflections did not stick. I was once again a pessimist.

The day after Reds Meadows we were faced with twenty-eight miles before reaching Tuolumne Meadows. It was a major stop for most hikers in the heart of Yosemite National Park. It had a general store, a grill, and most importantly, a post office. We knew family and friends had sent food to the post office. Since it closed at 5:00 p.m., we also knew we had to walk fast to make it before the deadline. On a normal day, we didn't give ourselves a deadline, and didn't have a quota for miles, but that day we had both. It added to the stress our hunger and exhaustion were already putting on our mind and bodies.

The miles that day weren't any harder or easier than the previous miles in Central California. We still had to navigate tough climbs and mountain passes. Luckily, the final miles into Tuolumne were either downhill or flat as we made our way through the meadows.

It was then, as Optimist and I tried to power walk through the last miles, that I started to go a little crazy. My mind started to break down from all the stress of getting the day's miles in before 5:00 p.m. At one point during the last flat miles, my brain moved faster than my feet could carry me, and I tripped on my own slow feet, landing flat on my face. I wasted no time in popping up and nearly running down the trail, our deadline looming.

Overall, I'm a fairly laid back person. I don't get stressed over little things, I don't particularly care what other people think about me, and I try to go with the flow. Putting all that aside, put a deadline in front of me, or an end goal with time constraints, and I become a different person. Suddenly all I can think about is getting to that end goal given my parameters. It becomes my obsession. That day, getting to the Tuolumne Meadows post office before it closed was my life focus. Nothing else mattered. I was not ok with achieving anything less. There was no convincing me otherwise of what the day's plan should be.

It made me miserable. Once I had the carrot dangling in front of me, I shut off my peripheral and could only see two feet ahead of me. I never once took in the amazing scenery or enjoyment that those twenty-eight miles offered me. I'm not even sure I spoke to Optimist at all that day.

By the time we were in our final miles, it wasn't looking good. We only had about a half hour left with about three miles to go. Most people struggle to run three miles in thirty minutes, much less walk that fast. There was no way we would make it. To make matters worse, not only did we temporarily lose the trail for about five minutes, we also found that the store was over a mile further away than indicated in the guidebook.

When we arrived to where we thought the store should have been, we found ourselves crossing a bridge and running into a cluster of cabins, but no store. We saw a road and a lot of cars, but still no store. It was maddening.

Since it was a popular part of the park, there were plenty of weekenders milling around the area near the trail. We stopped a group of three women and asked them where the store was (by now it was around 4:55 p.m.), and they replied, "Oh, it's about a mile down that way," as they pointed further down the trail.

I cracked.

"No! The book says it's supposed to be right here! That's impossible! We can't have another mile! It should be right here!"

I yelled back into their stunned faces as I pointed to the book and caused everyone around us to pause to watch the scene I was making.

These people had no idea what book I was referring to and no idea why I was yelling at them for the store not being right there. They just knew that I was a complete stranger, dirty, skinny and ragged looking, yelling at them for something entirely out of their control. They were just outside for a mere stroll in the park, doing us a favor by giving us directions. I poured all my stress and anger back on them. They gave me a look that affirmed that I was having a mental lapse, and quickly walked away from us.

While I was livid because we still had another mile, Optimist was angry at my behavior. He gave me the same look of disbelief and shock that the strangers had, and continued to walk alone towards the store. He didn't say a word to me as he walked away.

He eventually stopped after a half mile to sit on a log along the side of the trail, contemplating what to do with me and my tantrums. I could see it in his face that I had gotten to him. He admitted that my negativity was finally cracking him. He wouldn't continue the trail with me if I was going to have a breakdown every time we entered a town, or every day that we had a deadline. He was tired of my fuming and blowing up at strangers. He was ready to go it alone on the trail rather than feel like he was dragging me through it.

I was ready to quit. There was nothing I wanted more than to take the next bus out of the park, book a flight home, and call it an attempt at a thru-hike. There was nothing he could do to make me enjoy the experience. It wasn't fair for me to expect him to be able to do that, even if he wanted to. I couldn't ask him to be responsible for both of our states of minds. I needed to take ownership of my own happiness, and that became all the more apparent at that moment. I realized that he was better off alone and without me if I was going to keep going down this path of self-destruction. I had to get my act together if we were going to make it, not only to Canada, but also as a couple.

It was an important moment for us as we sat there along the side of the trail. To the other people just passing by, we looked like two hikers just taking a rest on a log. To us, it was a major fork in the road. I had to make my choice not only about staying on the trail, but also about my attitude. I couldn't keep falling into the trap of letting so many outside influences determine my happiness. In doing so, I felt like ropes were tied around my waist, pulling me in so many different directions, changing my mood all the time. In reality, I had the ability to pull right back on those ropes and control my emotions so that even though I couldn't choose when the ropes pulled on me, I could control my reactions to their pull, not allowing them to decide my outlook on life.

Sitting on the log, looking at Optimist, I knew which path I wanted to pursue, yet I was still overwhelmed by just how darn hard the trail was. I got up and started walking again while Optimist stayed on the log. I thought through my decision alone. I wanted so badly to choose the trail life with Optimist. I wanted to promise him I would work towards choosing my happiness rather than letting the trail rule me. I knew that making the choice would still be hard, but I wanted nothing more than to be with Optimist. I no longer wanted to impede his own happiness with my unhappiness.

Despite these thoughts, I was still a work in progress as I continued to walk.

It was a really long time before I had any other major breakdowns. I still had small mental lapses where I just wasn't in the mood to walk, or was craving a particular food so badly that I wanted to scream. Optimist had those moments too, where the day seemed to drag for him as well, and the excitement just wasn't there.

Honestly, a thru-hike is a lot of walking all day long. It can get to be a little repetitive. It's hard for people to fathom just how much walking is involved in a thru-hike. When ten hours each day is spent doing just that, it's like having a full-time job (and then some) solely devoted to walking. And it's not just easy, mosey-at-your-own-pace walking. It's tough hiking up and down mountains, over rocks, roots and streams. Thru-hiking a long-distance trail really is a life that is unimaginable until it's put into practice.

My fourth major mental breakdown wasn't until Central Oregon, in the lava rock fields around the Three Sisters and Bend area. Luckily it was the least major of all my mental breakdowns, and it only lasted the length of several miles through a lava rock section.

Though the area was beautiful and relatively flat, I hated the terrain. If you have ever hiked on lava rocks, you know that it's very difficult. The footing isn't stable because your feet are always slipping as rocks are moving beneath them. It's like running on soft sand. You extend a lot of effort yet seem to go nowhere. My hiking poles were useless in helping me navigate the lava rocks, as the tips of the poles wedged themselves between the rocks. I'd be walking and would suddenly be slung back as the tip of my poles got stuck and wouldn't allow me to move forward. I'd yank my poles out before continuing on, leaving a few profanities in my wake.

Optimist adjusted fine to the terrain, and at that point we were hiking around another thru-hiker, Jen, who was a fast hiker. They covered ground much faster than me. I knew the moment I set foot on the lava rocks, I would be annoyed. I told them to go on ahead and pick a camp spot for the night while I fought off my mental demons through the lava rocks.

As I hiked alone, I was angry at the trail for having such a difficult section to hike. I felt like it created itself that way just to give me a hard time, and I yelled loudly at the trail as I made my way through it. There was no one there to hear me, nor did I care if they did.

Tears streamed down my face, the wind whipped my hair around and it stuck to my wet cheeks. Trees didn't grow well in lava rocks, so there wasn't much to block the winds as they churned around me, making the section all the more difficult.

I wanted to punch someone for creating such a trail and leading it right through lava fields. All I wanted was an easy detour back to soft ground in the belly of trees. I hated that I was so clumsy and inept compared to other hikers over difficult terrain. It was another low moment, and I'm glad I was alone.

The difference between this breakdown and the previous ones was that I knew it was a breakdown. I knew I was choosing to let the trail get to me. It wasn't an impossible section to enjoy or to walk through. Optimist and Jen were having a great time chatting as their feet glided seemingly effortlessly over the rocks (at least from my perspective). I was simply ok at that point in choosing to wallow in self-pity as I fumbled my way over the rocks and cursed aloud, knowing my lapse would be over shortly but being fully immersed in it as it happened.

By the time we made it to Washington, I thought I was through with mental breakdowns. We only had about 500 miles left and were in our final twenty days on the trail. It seemed like nothing could stop us from finishing. That was until I learned the term "knife-edge".

In the middle of Washington there was a section called the Goat Rocks Wilderness. Even today, each time I hear its name, I tense up just remembering the section. The name certainly sounds normal with goats, rocks and wilderness, but there are a few more words that should always be included when describing that section of the trail. Words like knife-edge, narrow, steep, and loose rock. The list goes on with words that I came up with when describing the real Goat Rocks Wilderness.

I first heard the term knife-edge a day before we reached the section. We ran into a group of four hikers that were out for a week's camping trip. They had chosen to hike the section through Goat Rocks because they'd heard what an amazing views the hike offered. The group described slipping on the snow, being scared, and hating the knife-edge portion of the section. I thought they were being overly dramatic because they were just out there for the week and out of shape. I'd seen everything the trail could throw at me and felt like a machine. That was until I walked the knife-edge.

The beginning of the section started off with fairly easy hiking. It was like any other section of the trail along a ridgeline, with the trail being carved into the side of the mountain. Sure, there were some loose rocks, and a section with slippery snow, but it wasn't terrible. Then the trail did something I hadn't yet experienced. It walked over the crest of the mountain and dropped off on both sides.

Hence the term, knife-edge.

As I walked the crest, the wind swirled around me. I was exposed to the cross-winds and thick clouds moving quickly over the mountain. It wouldn't have been bad had it been a flat walk. But, mountains are not flat. While the trail dropped off on both sides, leaving me little room for error in my choice of steps, it also climbed and dropped over the tops of the mountains.

I was already a slow hiker, so when it came to this section, I slowed down even more. I watch every step, scared of making one wrong move and ending it all for real. Optimist started running the trail, excited at the 360 degree views from atop the mountain and loving the newly added element of danger.

It was to my demise that I moved so slowly, because the trail was composed of loose gravel. It offered terrible footing and going slower made it worse. I fell on my butt twice because my feet slipped out from under me, not only raising my heart rate because I was so close to the edge, but also raising my emotions to an unbearable level. I started tearing up and shaking uncontrollably. I wanted more than ever to be off the trail and in the comfort and safety of my home. I clutched the first cluster of rocks I reached and stopped walking. I had tensed up beyond the point of forward movement.

I was frozen there on the trail as I cried and watched Optimist get further and further away. As I watched him run along the trail, never fearing the terrain, I was angry. How could he enjoy this so much, and what was I doing with a guy that found enjoyment in situations that I cursed and feared? I sat and questioned that until I could no longer see Optimist in the distance. After a few minutes, I started walking again. My mind knew it was the only way off the mountain, and my vision was clouded with tears as I was once again cussing aloud, cursing anyone who ever had to do with creating the trail.

As I made my way over the crest, focused only on living through those miles, I contemplated ending the trail and my relationship with Optimist. Our four years together meant very little to me at that moment. I knew that this wouldn't be the only adventure we would have. He wanted a life full of adventures just like this, adventures that might be even more challenging, both mentally and physically. I knew that by choosing to stay on the trail, I was choosing a life full of experiences just like this one. I knew that the effort I was making to choose to be happy despite negative circumstances would be an effort I might make many more times in a life with Optimist. At that point, as I looked at the sheer drops just inches away from my feet, I wanted to hit the escape button and just end it all by getting off the trail in the next town. I no longer cared if I was within a couple of weeks of finishing a thru-hike. The end goal no longer mattered. I didn't care if I could claim victory at overcoming all obstacles to complete the entire walk.

When I finally met up with Optimist, when the trail returned to safe ridgeline, and I was out of the whipping wind and foreboding drops on either side, I found him sitting off the side of the trail. He was talking with two men who had just finished the same section a few minutes before us. I wiped away my tears and tried to act happy to them. I didn't want to show my weakness.

They were tangibly excited to meet thru-hikers. We were celebrities to them and I was breaking apart on the inside.

After talking with them for a bit, they reached into their packs and gave us fresh bell peppers, carrots, and packaged trail meals. They planned on hiking out to town that day and didn't need all the extra food, so they wanted us to have it. Their visible admiration of us tore me up inside. I was scared they would learn my secret that I had an extremely difficult time passing the mental test that the trail so often provided. I felt guilty being seen as a rock of strength, but was crumbling on the inside because of my own self-destructive thoughts and actions. To them I was different, but to me I was just as human and easily breakable as the next person.

I felt like a hypocrite after we walked away from the men and headed further down the trail. I was ashamed at the choices I had made during those last few miles. Just moments before meeting them I had been stuck in my own mind and my own self-pity. I had contemplated quitting because I downright couldn't handle the challenge. Complete strangers who had just hiked the same section right before me took the opportunity to help us simply because we were thru-hikers. They looked at us with reverence in their eyes, and I was cursing the trail and all that it included. I had bet they would have given anything to be in our position, to have the sole responsibility of walking from Mexico to Canada. Yet there I was, completely ungrateful for the life that so few ever have the chance to live.

I did not quit that day. Once out of danger, I was able to think more logically once again and continue walking. I'm not proud of that last mental breakdown, but I was at least able to interpret it into a useful purpose. By the end of the trail, I knew the choice to be happy was mine to make, and I knew I could not let outside influences rule my emotions. It was always difficult to employ that lesson, but the fact that I knew it was there to practice was a big step for me. I realized that I wasn't just a pinball being tossed around in life. I had a choice of which path I took when different situations were presented to me.

Despite my moments on insanity, there were in fact times along the trail when I took a step back to look at all the options laid out before me rather than reacting with emotional, often illogical decisions that ultimately left me depressed. Those were the times when I realized that everything was not in my control, and that it simply couldn't be. The sooner I accepted that, the sooner I figured out that my reactions were solely all my own.

When situations were out of our control, like the trail being littered with cow and horse poop, we had a choice as to how to react to those circumstances. I cursed them mercilessly, upset that I had to share the trail with other living beings such as cows, or I deftly and gingerly avoided them.

They were simply a part of the life that came with the trail. We also avoided camping near them, as they truly were a gross presence on the trail.

As it is with most situations in life, just as I was deeply disturbed by how I reacted to the previously described ones, I'm also proud of how I reacted to others.

Though nature rewarded us with water in Central California, the water's abundance led to the presence of one of our least favorite things about the entire trail: mosquitoes. They were everywhere. I grew up in Ohio, with hot, humid summers full of mosquitoes. The ankle-biting, didn't slap your leg soon enough before it drew blood, while you're trying to enjoy a cool evening on the back porch, annoying mosquitoes. All the mosquitoes I experienced in my first twenty-five years of life did not add up to the army of mosquitoes I fought in Central California.

Because we were constantly surrounded by water, a lot of it standing water, we were also surrounded by mosquitoes. They buzzed in our ears, our eyes, our noses, and our mouths, threatening to suck any available source of blood. We involuntarily swatted all the time we walked, killing them as they buzzed in mid-air in front of us, slapping our faces and necks, mixing their dead bodies with our layers of dirt, sunscreen and sweat. Our killing sprees were not enough to defeat them. There were just too many of them.

The mosquitoes' presence was completely out of our control. All we could do was adapt our lifestyle to living with them. We covered our skin with any fabric available, including pants, jackets, hats, sunglasses and bandannas. We even wore our thin gloves and long socks. Optimist and I were both a sweaty mess at the end of each day, having been bundled up for the heat of the day. It was worth the shield we created from the mosquitoes. Our hiking days started earlier too. An earlier start meant we beat mosquitoes to the wakeup call of dawn. Still, we could always hear their faint buzzing in the cool morning air.

Higher elevation meant cooler nights and fewer mosquitoes, so we sought out those campsites each day, allowing us to avoid at least some of the bugs. Snack breaks and meals were greatly shortened. As soon as we stopped moving, the mosquitoes were ready to pounce. They searched out any available food source on our bodies, relentless in their search for unprotected skin. We even developed a tent entrance routine, where Optimist flapped his sleeping pad, a thin mattress, in the air by the tent door as I quickly zipped open the tent and flung myself and our gear in. We created enough air current so the mosquitoes couldn't follow me in. He waved his mattress feverishly before giving me the signal to zip open the door so he could then throw himself in and yell, "I'm in!" to signal for me to zip the door shut. We'd then sit calmly, listening for any stray mosquitoes that happened to follow us in, ready to crush them before they got to us.

It was a battle with the mosquitoes and we fought hard.

Neither side really won. There was no way we could obliterate their population. All they really did was drive us crazy with their buzzing and biting. What was important was that while the mosquitoes' presence was entirely out of our control, we adapted ourselves such that we could live through them without being driven too crazy, and without losing too much blood.

Another element completely out of our control was the weather. Luckily we didn't have to think about the weather until we were well into the trail. Sure, it was hot and dry in Southern California and both hot and cool in Central and Northern California, but the sky was always blue above our heads. It wasn't until the state of Washington that we realized just how great clear skies were, heat or no heat. Precipitation was a real downer when hiking a long-distance trail.

Rain for a thru-hiker is difficult. Gear gets wet, clothes get soaked, and overall, everything feels cold and damp. And that's only from one day of rain. String a few days of rain together, and it's downright miserable. A tent is the one piece of gear that will always get wet in the rain. It's actually exposed to the rain on purpose, to keep the hiker and all the gear dry under its cover. Since everything is crammed together in a pack, things are bound to get wet if one item is completely soaked. That would be how our tent was.

Washington was a state with volatile, change-in-a-minute-weather. Near the middle of the state, it started raining and didn't stop for three days. I don't remember when it began and I don't remember when it ended. I just know that for three straight days, we set up and took down camp in the rain, we took snack and meal breaks in the rain, and we trudged in the mud and rain. My shoes, thoroughly soaked, squished and bubbled through their mesh outer layer with every step I took. Though we sought out dry spots under dense tree branches, we were constantly fighting to keep our gear dry.

The rain fly on the outside of the tent could only do so much before it got soaked, being the first layer of defense. Once it was wet, it leaked into the second layer, our tent walls. Our tent was eventually wet through every stitch of fabric. The combination of cold, wet tent walls and warm bodies caused condensation and created droplets of water all over the inside of the tent. The inside being where we were trying to keep our bodies and other gear dry.

Because of the presence of water everywhere, inside and out, I was very cautious in avoiding any contact with the tent walls. They meant moisture, a constant threat to my dry, warm being. You may be picturing a mansion of a tent, but with Optimist and I, and both our packs, our bodies were just a few inches from each side and the roof of the tent. We could barely sit up without our heads touching the top. We constantly reminded each other, "Don't touch the walls!"

It was incredibly difficult to stay positive throughout those three days of rain. We were surrounded by dense fog and low-lying clouds without so much as a break in the weather. All the things that I had previously enjoyed about the trail, like snack breaks and meals, were much more difficult. We found the driest spots available, knowing some raindrops would find their way through the thickest of leaves and branches. Once we did find places to stop and eat, my body temperature would drop immediately as I sat still. My whole body would shake to its core and my teeth would chatter after resting for even a few minutes. Temperatures were in the low fifties, and we carried little clothing as it was. Even if I wore every layer of clothing that I carried, they'd still get soaking wet and do nothing for my warmth. There were times when I contemplated the pros and cons of warming my hands in the fire from the stove. Sure it would hurt, but it would be oh so warm!

The longer the rain continued, the more the water soaked through every thread of our tent, and the damper all the other contents of our packs became. I kept my sleeping bag in a garbage bag in order to create another layer between the wet tent and my precious source of warmth. If my sleeping bag ever got wet, I was doomed. It was my only hope of warmth and comfort at the end of a long, wet, bone-chilling day. It was the one saving grace. Clothes weren't the only key to staying warm at night. I could at least be naked in my sleeping bag and still be warm.

Though it was difficult to stay positive, it was just as difficult to become completely negative. Just like the mosquitoes, I knew the weather was so far removed from my grasp of control. Though it wasn't forgiven, it was simply excused. I could do nothing to influence the weather. All I could do was prepare myself and my pack to stay both sane and dry. It was the only rational choice.

There were other choices, like getting angry or upset at the clouds that simply wouldn't move from above our heads. By that point, I had already found that being angry at such things helped nothing. Being negative only drug me further down in the cold, wet, dark tunnel of pessimism. Being positive, or at least logical enough to see ways to make life a little better while dealing with something as uncontrollable as the rain, let me see past the grainy details and into the grand picture. I could see that the only way to make the situation better, more livable and more enjoyable, was to make choices that led to alleviating the situation rather than shoving the discomforts back into my face. I chose the former over the latter, and that is how I made it through three straight days of rain in Washington.

Washington was also a difficult state because of the previous years' volatile weather. In 2003, violent storms damaged a forty-five mile section of the trail, causing that part of the trail to be nearly impassable. Bridges were washed out from rivers raging with both rain and snow melt, mud slides caused some of the trail to simply fall off the side into nonexistence, and hundred-year-old trees were blown down and piled on top of each other.

That part of the trail had been nearly untouched since 2003. Since nature worked quickly to reclaim its land, the trail was not only hard to follow, but also nonexistent at some points. There had been an established detour to the original route, which hikers had been taking for the few years leading up to our hike. In the year of our hike, the detour section caught fire. Thus, a detour to the detour section was created. This time it was a fifty-mile road walk.

A road walk might sound good at first hearing. For us it meant a section that was dangerous from speeding cars, boring from a lack of scenery, and difficult from extremely hard asphalt on already tired legs. We simply didn't like our options of a section with a torn up trail, a section on fire, or a section on the road. The time to make a choice of which section to hike was fast approaching after we entered the state of Washington on day ninety. We had known about this section since day one and had hoped that an answer would present itself somewhere during the days leading up to the section.

Rather than risk the fire on the detour (our last option, really), or the long road walk, we braved the original section. It was a strange feeling to enter the closed section. There was a "point of no return" sign in the middle of the trail, warning of the trail ahead and advising a detour. It felt like we were walking into a battle in which we knew we would not get out unscathed. The trail was even symbolic in that after a few miles of easy terrain, a calming before the storm, it swept downhill into a dark bowl of thick tree growth. My chest tightened and my legs felt weak as we eyed it from a distance. As we moved closer to the thick-growth section, I could feel it close around us. It sealed its entrance behind us and stretched out a gauntlet ahead of us, challenging us to make it out the other side. At that point it was just Optimist and I, and we knew there weren't many hikers, if any, ahead of us. We knew that the pack ahead of us took the road walk, and we weren't sure of anyone behind us. I couldn't have imagined hiking it alone.

The first river crossing, the White Chuck River, took forty-five minutes to cross. It should have normally taken about ten seconds on a bridge. I shouldn't have looked at my watch to time it, but I couldn't help myself. It only made it a realization that the section was going to be long and laborious, and that we were going to have to work hard for every step. The river was raging angrily, too deep in every spot to simply wade across, and the current too strong to even let us try. We followed pink ribbons that were tied to trees down to a spot where we thought we were supposed to cross, the broken bridge looming twenty feet above our heads. Optimist tried out several rocks, getting stuck in the middle of the river every time, unable to find a pattern in the second half of the river's rocks in order to make it across. I stood there frozen on the river bank, unable to think of another way to cross and unable to watch Optimist for fear that he could fall in with one bad step.

We eventually ditched the rocks when we saw there was no passable way across them, and moved further downstream along the river. We hoped for another path of rocks or for calmer waters. The water only gathered more momentum as it followed us downstream, looking more hopeless as my watch ticked on loudly in my ear, minutes passing with the setting sun. Then we saw more pink ribbons. We had stopped following them too early. They led us further downstream, eventually to a large tree lying on its side, spanning the width of the river.

It was our only hope of getting across. The tree log sat just a couple of feet above the swift-moving water, and was too slippery and too round to walk across. Optimist army-crawled across it, carefully balancing his pack across his back. The pack is a huge deterrent in keeping the body balanced, as it is weight beyond the self. It's easily capable of swaying a person's weight once it decides to go its own way. I still have nightmares of watching Optimist crawl across the log. I'm afraid that his pack will shift, causing him to fall into the swift moving current, carrying him downstream, never to be seen again.

I opted for scooting across the log, straddling it tightly with my arms and legs as my whole body shook with nerves. I had to look down to make sure that my body moved in unison across the log. Looking down also meant watching the water move swiftly beneath me, waiting for me to make a mistake.

Optimist and I learned a lot from that first crossing. We realized that the section was going to take patience, time and a lot more effort. Looking at watches, stressing about miles, and lapses in mental strength were temporarily banned, as if they should be allowed anyway on the trail. We weren't going to just breeze through the last few days on the trail as we had originally planned. Miles that normally took fifteen to twenty minutes to walk took nearly an hour each.

The blow-downs also proved to be a great test of patience. Imagine trees as wide as five to ten feet in diameter, lying on their sides like big matchsticks, one on top of another. They required climbing over and above, lifting oneself and one's pack weight. They are not piles of trees one can simply hop over.

Just before the Sitkum Creek crossing, the same night as the White Chuck River, I got so tangled in the maze of blow-downs, unable to go over or under them and trying to squeeze my way through, that even my pack got stuck. I had to take it off and heave it through the branches before wiggling my own body through tangles of trees and branches. Later down the trail, we climbed over trees that were lying across the trail, one on top of the other, stretching several feet above our heads. The trees were hundreds of years old, their girth spanning wider than our height. Piling several on top of each other caused quite an obstacle course. All the time, we were trying to stay on the seemingly invisible trail while maneuvering over the piles. We had several more difficult river crossings, mudslides that required scooting down a mere remnant of the trail, and thick overgrowth of weeds that suffocated both us and the trail.

There was no way I would have made it through that section had I chosen to react negatively to the difficulties laid ahead of us. I would have turned on Optimist just as before, angry with our one mile per hour pace.

I was relieved when we crossed the last test of the gauntlet, the Suiattle River, but was also pleased that I kept my head above the madness. For once, I didn't let the section swallow me whole or tear me apart. It wasn't the happiest or most enjoyable part of the trail, but I chose to react positively to a negative situation.

Those moments of positive reactions were different from mental breakdowns because in my moments of insanity, I wanted to blame other factors for my shortfalls, for my inability to navigate the trail. When I knew it was fruitless to blame something out of my control, like the weather, I was more adept in choosing my happiness and simply moving up the trail.

The ultimate lesson I learned on the entire Pacific Crest Trail is that I have a choice when it comes to my happiness. No one else can choose it for me, and no one is making me choose either way. The decision is mine to make, the reaction is my own, and my attitude is in my control.

I can name hundreds of times along the trail when I either employed this lesson or blatantly ignored it. If we're talking about real life, increase that number at least ten-fold. This lesson is on one hand so pervasive in our everyday lives that it practically slaps us in the face. On the other hand, it is so subtle that it's like an ocean's undercurrent, ready to pull us under if we're not paying attention. It is easily ignored or downright forgotten, to our own demise. All too often we attribute our unhappiness to factors outside of ourselves.

I am far from fully living this lesson in my everyday life, from choosing my own happiness. I know it's there for me to practice. I strive to achieve it, to accept the fact that I have the choice in my own life's happiness. Despite my efforts, often it's easier not to make the choice, to say that my life's happiness it outside of my hands. I often blame my unhappiness on any one of the millions of life-stressors constantly circling me. I allow outside factors to choose my happiness for me, like pressure at work, bad relationships with family members, or concerns about money. I always want that escape button. Unfortunately the escape button doesn't lead to happiness.

When I choose to be the eye of the storm, the calm among the chaos, I am most happy. I know the stressors swirling around me, but I make the decision to be happy outside of their existence. I know I'm separate from any other person or factor that tries to impose its negativity on me. It's at those moments when I realize that my life's surroundings mean nothing towards my own happiness or unhappiness. They are just objects existing at the same moment as my own life, not working towards or against me. The trail did not exist to make my life better or worse. It simply existed at the same time I chose to live three months of my life on it.

When I realized that despite whatever the environment around me might be, despite what the people near me might say or do, that I could still make the choice to be happy, I was free. I was free from the fear of not being happy in any given situation. I assured myself that I could live and choose happiness in any given country, climate or culture. Yes, it takes adjusting when things change, and there are less than desirable places to live due to location and lifestyle, but part of that adjustment is the choices we make when presented with change.

One distinction that many people miss in this lesson is the difference between control of the situation and choice of reactions to the situation. I cannot control everything that happens to me. I cannot control nature or other people's choices or actions. But, when something out of my control happens to me, I have a choice in how I react to those outside influences. This lesson is not implying that I can plan for every event in my life, thus creating happiness that way. This lesson is saying that I can make lemonade with whatever lemons I've been given. I can create a beautiful life out of seemingly ugly ingredients.

I talked about this lesson with a friend recently. His daughter is currently earning her PhD in biology at Harvard. He has seen her devote the last several years of her life to be at this point, in the top of her field. It has not been easy for her, and it has not been without pitfalls. But, to outsiders walking into her life at this particular point, they only see her at the top. They do not see all the hard work she's put in to get there. They only see her current success. To them, it's as if her success fell into her lap and she caught it. The reality is that she's fought hard to be where she is at right now, and has many more battles to stay at the top.

After hearing about my friend's daughter, it hit me that most people who appear to have it "easy", to have been dealt the best of cards, are most likely people who are living out this lesson. They did not figure out the secret to controlling their life's path. Rather, they realized the control they have in choosing happiness down any given path. It only looks easy for them because they've created a life such that when a roadblock presents itself, they look around and see hundreds of other roads leading to the same end goal of happiness. Rather than whine, kick and scream so everyone knows how unhappy they are, they've chosen a positive reaction before anyone even notices the negative situation they overcame. They don't dwell on telling others what a hard life they have because they're too busy making choices to be happy with what they're given.

On the trail, I freed myself from the self-destruction that chained me during my mental breakdowns when I stepped back from the small details and looked at myself. I saw that with changes in life come choices, and with choices comes the power to decide. The power lies in knowing that the choice is solely mine to make at any given point. Choosing to give up the power to make a choice and attributing unhappiness to outside factors is still a choice. Many people, me included, often make the choice of giving up the power to decide. Yet, that doesn't mean it's not possible to choose the other less traveled path of happiness. Happiness is not given and it is not found, but rather, it's chosen.

You always have a choice.

11 LIFE AFTER CANADA

What does one do after thru-hiking the PCT?

As you already know, there was no welcome party at the finish. No balloons, no pizza and no ice cream. No one that we met in Canada knew about the trail, nor cared to learn how we got there or why we were so filthy. It was a quick transition back into the real world where others don't take much interest in strangers. And that was all on the same day that I finished my grand hike of 109 days on the trail. The celebration was a party of two, Optimist and Stopwatch.

Within just two days of finishing, Matt and I rode a bus from Vancouver, Canada to Seattle, Washington, and then flew on a plane to Ohio. Since we were back in the real world, we were Matt and Julie once again. And, since we didn't have jobs or any real obligations, we spent a week with family in Ohio, mainly eating, sleeping and telling stories to wide-eyed listeners.

It was very strange.

For over three months straight, my days consisted of waking up to the sky above my head, to walking all day with my life on my back, and to being in close-quarters only with myself and Matt. Suddenly I was waking up in a bed, with a roof over my head, with food and drink seemingly limitless, surrounded by family members and a city of people, and most importantly, with no miles to walk. It was both very strange and very sad. Strange because my life shifted so quickly, and sad because my trail life really was over. I finally realized what a great experience I just had and that I may never have again. I finally fell in love with the trail life.

After that, all I wanted was to be back on the trail. The trail that I hated for so long, that I cursed under my breath so many times, that broke me mentally and physically each day. I yearned for the life I lived on the trail. I wanted the simplicity back. I wanted those quiet mornings when I was walking in the clean, crisp air with just the sound of my own feet crunching the ground and the thoughts in my head. I wanted my possessions to fit in a bag on my back, and I wanted to be eating a warm bowl of noodles with just Matt and a campfire.

Within days of finishing, every part of me wanted to be back on the trail. Yet, as I knew the truth in my situation, that wasn't possible. Our adventure on the PCT was over, and I was left with my own regrets of not fully embracing each privileged day that I spent on it. It was time to move on to the next lifestyle back in the real world of jobs, bills and responsibilities beyond walking.

After my initial detoxification from the trail, I continued my life with Matt as we moved to the West Coast, to Vancouver, Washington. We live just forty-five minutes from the PCT. That certainly wasn't the plan while hiking the trail, but became a reality after a job for Matt brought us back west, almost magnetically.

Since finishing the trail we have lived quite normally, at least on the surface. We work office jobs on the weekdays, enjoy our two-day weekends, save our money, live in an apartment, and chug right along with everyone else on this similar life path. Yet, both Matt and I know we are different from our peers. There is a fire below our surfaces that gives us strength, and that gives us an edge on those around us. We know this isn't the only life possible. Other lives exist beyond the nine to five, beyond the meetings and deadlines, beyond the grind and commercial push to consume.

While it may be our life right now, there are endless other choices, and the choices are all ours. We have a deep knowledge of both ourselves and the world that can only be gained through challenging experiences such as thru-hiking the PCT. The PCT was such a raw experience that its lessons felt like a cold shower in the dead of winter. The trail shook me to my core. It was impossible to ignore the lessons, and the only way to escape them was to quit the trail.

While these same lessons are prevalent in everyday life experiences, they are on such a low volume that few of us actually have good enough ears to hear them. Contrast that to the trail life, where the lessons were so loud that I would have needed ear plugs to block them out. Case in point: pooping my pants. I'd say it was a pretty obvious example of practicing humility. I wasn't just slapped in the face with that lesson. I got shit on by the lesson, and by my own self. When was the last time you were humbled to that extent in real life? We all seem pretty important in our own bubbles, and it's rare that those bubbles get popped to expose the even larger bubble of the world.

Going through life on the commonly unexamined life path simply doesn't teach the same lessons as those that we learned while walking. Perhaps it's possible to be done, but one would have to dig pretty deep to unearth the lessons otherwise. It's just the nature of the ease we've created in our lives, with fresh water at our fingertips, grocery stores on every corner, and cars in the garage to take us there. There is nothing wrong with those enhancements in life. However, they certainly don't lend themselves to teaching us core lessons that give us a greater appreciation for their presence or a deeper understanding of ourselves.

Not a day goes by that I don't think about the trail. Every part of my life was touched by thru-hiking the PCT. I can't turn on the bathroom faucet to brush my teeth without thinking of how sparse water was on the trail, endless aisles of food at the grocery store seem like a cruel joke in remembering my hunger, and my daily seven-mile run is a piece of cake compared to the twenty-five mile average I logged while carrying upwards of forty pounds on my back. Life just seems too easy off the trail.

Yet, it's that much harder. My life is so much more complicated compared to my daily to-do list on the trail of walk, eat and sleep. I'm surrounded by an apartment full of stuff that would take a large moving truck to contain, my relationship with family members could always be better, I'm stressed by the responsibilities and pressure loaded on me at work, and I question my happiness every day.

While I can fully articulate the lessons I learned while hiking the PCT, and I know how those experiences can be applied to my daily life, I still struggle in living them out. The bottom line is that it's just too easy to ignore them. It's easy to take for granted that I'm well off enough that water and food are not resources that are hard to come by or that need rationing. Stuff accumulates, like clothes in my closet, nearly effortlessly. Keeping friendships to a minimum, in both number of friends and efforts to keep them, comes naturally to me. This is often to my detriment and loneliness once I realize I've pushed away most everyone I know. It's hard to see or spread goodness in the world when the news is mainly comprised of bad people doing terrible acts against their own species, nor does my mind gravitate to random acts of kindness. Using my senses isn't commonplace in my bland, concrete and plastic surroundings. I'm a big fish in my own sea, of which I rarely leave to see that my sea is a mere droplet of water in the really big sea of the world. Leaving the comfort of the herd, of the middle-class America that works office jobs all day with weekends off, is much harder to do than I originally thought. Lastly, knowing that happiness is a choice and actually making that choice are two entirely different concepts, of which I'm terrible in living out the latter.

Still, I know the lessons are there. I know the worth in living them. I know how greatly life can be enhanced by fully embracing them. I know that I can live like I'm on the trail without physically being out there. Each and every moment is an opportunity to make a choice. Recognizing the worth in each lesson is a choice, as is practicing each lesson.

For me, choosing to be happy is by far the hardest choice for me to make. I can think of so many reasons, so many excuses, of why I choose otherwise. I'm tired, my job is stressful, and it has been pouring down rain for three weeks straight. While these are situations that lend themselves to a less than desirable life, they are not making me choose to be unhappy. They are simply present at the same moment that I am living, just as the trail existed at the same time as me. But, the trail never made me feel anything. I chose to be unhappy as a reaction to the difficulties that the trail presented, just as I choose in my present life to be unhappy because of everyday life stressors of to-do lists, bills, and other people. Nothing is in my control but my own choice. That is the phrase that I remind myself of on a daily, if not moment to moment, basis.

While I'm reminded of all these lessons on a daily basis through my memories of the trail and my day to day experiences, my goal is not necessarily to be perfect in living the lessons. It would be just as wrong to have that goal as it was for me to start the PCT with just the goal of walking from Mexico to Canada. My goal is the experience in between the bookends, knowing that the experience will have ups and downs, but that I'll be all the more fulfilled living out every moment. I cannot relive the past, and I cannot solely focus on the future, but I can be fully present, making a choice in every thought and action.

Writing this book has helped me realize the worth in an adventure such as hiking the PCT. I would not be the same person, nor would I want to know that person, had I not thru-hiked the trail. These lessons may have taken my whole life to bring forth. I feel privileged that I was able to learn them while still in my twenties, and it only took a little over three months and 2600 miles to learn them. In the grand scheme of a lifetime, that's nothing. I still feel like a baby in the world, so sheltered and scared to face it. The rest of the world that I have yet to experience represents the unknown, and the unknown brings forth fears. When was the last time you willingly headed straight forward, full-speed ahead, into the unknown?

I doubt that answer is, "Each and every day."

There is still so much I don't know about myself, about others and about life. While it's intimidating, it's also exciting. Life is not finished. I am not finished. I have many more adventures ahead of me, and so many more lessons to learn.

Starting a new adventure is like running in the rain. The first five minutes are terrible, but after that, I don't even notice it. Once I'm done, I'm thankful I peeled my butt off the couch and burned some calories. The euphoria of finishing the run is worth every ounce of wet clothing on my body. Just like running in the rain, it's both difficult and scary to leave the comfort of an easy, planned out life, yet I am so much better off once I'm in the thick of the experience and even at the end of it. Had I not stepped foot on the PCT, I would not have any of the previously described stories to tell. My life's glass of water would be severely under-filled.

While I fully tout the worth of the PCT, it is a challenge that few are able to take on. It is not for everyone, nor would I want everyone to try it. Again, it's just like running. I run about fifty miles a week, and I love it, but do I think everyone should run? No. Not everyone is mentally or physically wired for running. I'm just glad that no one makes me ride a bike two hours a day just because that's what they do for exercise and enjoyment. That would not be my cup of tea, as running is probably not theirs either.

I was lucky to be able to hike the PCT. My list of obligations were few, my calendar was wide open, and my ability to save money allowed for the financial obstacles of both paying for a thru-hike and not working to create incoming funds. I realize that not everyone's stars are aligned to hike the PCT. It's just not possible for the majority of people. But that is no excuse for not learning or living these lessons.

Just because most people can't hike the PCT doesn't mean they can't find those experiences that would make them step outside of their comfort zones.

Each one of us has our own bubble that we live in, that would be scary to leave. It's much easier to stay in that bubble than it is to look outside ourselves. Ironically, it is when we put ourselves out there, when factors are unknown, when life could be harder than we'd like it to be, that we really begin to know ourselves. Stepping outside of ourselves allows us to focus inward and clearly see what we're made of. When you are walking through the woods with only yourself to talk to, it's pretty hard to ignore your own thoughts when that's the only conversation you're having. It is inevitable that you will get to know yourself. Self-knowledge is perhaps one of our greatest fears when we don't have it, yet our greatest asset when we do.

These life lessons are not about the PCT. Strip away the trail, and you'll find that it's just another challenging experience beyond the drone of regular life. It's stepping outside the comfort zone and taking big risks but reaping big rewards. Without the PCT, you will still find the same lessons. The PCT was just that much more conducive to teaching me the lessons, but it's not the only way to learn them. It was simply my own way.

With that in mind, what is your PCT? What is that one adventure that scares you into slamming the front door shut and locking it, yet excites and entices you into looking through the door's peep hole to still see what's out there? What could lead you to have the same exciting experiences that would lead to a greater level of self-knowledge and mental clarity? What would make you look at life through a different pair of glasses, though it might scare you to even contemplate trying them on?

It is my hope that these stories from the trail have accurately portrayed life lessons worth living. It is my even greater hope that through my trials and errors in learning these lessons, you are motivated to have your own PCT adventure. Not that you will literally hike the trail, but that you will take that trepid step outside of yourself to also get to know yourself and the world better. That you too will see the worth in challenging life experiences that should otherwise deem you as unhappy, yet magically produce the opposite result because of the obstacles you overcame in getting from your Mexico to your Canada. Whatever your point A and point B may be, be sure to pay attention and pick up on what's going on in the middle, because that is where the lessons are learned and lived. It is where we make our choices. It is where life happens.

ACKNOWLEDGEMENTS

Many people have played a part in making my life, my experiences, and my thoughts, all possible. I cannot name them all, nor would I want to try, for fear of leaving someone out. Thru-hiking the trail and writing this book are just a small part of my life list that would have never been possible without someone there to encourage me. Thank you to all my family, my friends, and my Matt, for loving me or at least liking me, and supporting me. I know I don't always make it easy.

ABOUT THE AUTHOR

In addition to thru-hiking the Pacific Crest Trail, Julie has found herself in other life-changing experiences that started with her kicking and screaming and ended with her rising above the physical feats and the mental demons, coming out on top as a fulfilled person with an enriched life canvas. Originally from Cincinnati, Ohio, she has traveled through much of the U.S., whether on foot, via bicycle or in a car, and has lived in Addis Ababa, Ethiopia and traveled through the Simien Mountains, seeing places she would have never thought existed had she not pushed the boundaries of her comfort zone. She is an avid long-distance runner who appreciates the simple things in life, yet is always seeking a deeper meaning of herself, her place in this world, and her relationships with those around her. Matt Urbanski, her husband, is the force behind her and the impetus that lands her in such unique, challenging and otherwise dreary situations that always seem to end on a positive note of self-realization, mental strength, and the desire to do it all over again.

Made in the USA
Middletown, DE
25 September 2017